REAGAN'S REIGN OF ERROR

The Instant Nostalgia Edition

REAGAN'S REIGN OF ERROR

The Instant Nostalgia Edition

Mark Green and Gail MacColl

*with
Howard Gershen,
Robert Nelson,
Christopher Power,
and Michael
Vickerman*

*Pantheon Books
New York*

Library of Congress Cataloging-
in-Publication Data
Reagan's reign of error. Revised
edition of:
There he goes again.
    1. Reagan, Ronald—Quotations.
2. United States—Politics and
government—1981–
—Quotations, maxims, etc.
    I. Reagan, Ronald.   II. Green,
Mark J.   III. MacColl, Gail,
1954–   .   IV. Title: There he
goes again.
E838.5.R437 1987   973.927′092′4
87-19964 ISBN 0-394-75644-4

Photos pp. 1–6, 20–123, 176, UPI;
all others, AP/Wide World

Manufactured in the United States
of America

Revised Edition

To my loving and Republican parents—M. G.

To Mary Wentworth—G. M.

Authors' Note

The authors would like to give heartfelt thanks to those who so willingly contributed their time and expertise —without them this book simply would not have been possible. We thank: Susan Aasen, James Ainsworth, Ellen Battistelli, John Bickerman, Willie Blacklow, Ron Brownstein, Mike Calabrese, Adam Castro, Joan Claybrook, John Clewett, Neal Cohen, David Corbin, Tom Cosgrove, Steve Giardini, Debra Hall, Jay Harvey, Betsy Houghteling; Joseph Houghteling; Bill Johnston, Brian McCartan, Robert McIntyre, Keith McKeown, Victor Navasky, Stan Norris, Nan Richards, Martin Smith, Bill Spencer, Cecily Surace, Michael Waldman, and Janey Wright-Rutan. Public-policy institutes that proved especially helpful included: Americas Watch, Center for Defense Information, Center on Budget and Policy Priorities, Center for Study of Responsive Law, Congress Watch, Critical Mass, Greenpeace International, the National Clean Air Coalition, and the New York Civil Liberties Union. Equally helpful were ABC News, the staff of Wollman Library at Barnard College, the offices of Representatives George Miller and Pat Schroeder, the Senate Labor and Human Resources Committee, and the House Foreign Affairs Subcommittee on Arms Control, International Security, and Science.

Sources for quotes from Ronald Reagan are given in parentheses after each quote. "Radio" indicates that the quote was taken from transcripts of Mr. Reagan's nationally syndicated three-minute radio commentaries. Quotes from President Reagan, unless noted otherwise, are from *The Weekly Compilation of Presidential Documents,* a publication of the National Archives and Records Service, G.S.A.

TABLE OF CONTENTS

I will stand on, and continue to use, the figures I have used, because I believe they are correct. Now, I'm not going to deny that you don't now and then slip up on something; no one bats a thousand. (Philadelphia news conference, *Wash. Post,* 4/20/80)

INTRODUCTION:
To Err Is Reagan

—by Mark Green

"The speculation . . . has no foundation."

When Ronald Reagan spoke those words on November 6, 1986, to deny that his administration had sold arms to Iran, the Reagan era effectively came to a close. Yes, he could still veto bills and give speeches behind the presidential seal, but his magic spell was finally broken.

Looking back, it was something of a miracle that Reagan's credibility and sway survived even six years. From day one his standard operating procedure, as illustrated by his initial answer on arms to Iran, was a blend of ignorance, amnesia, and dissembling. Like a panicky passenger lunging for a life preserver, he would, under stress, concoct almost any fact or anecdote to advance his ideological beliefs. Ronald Reagan brought to mind Will Rogers' comment that "It's not what he doesn't know that bothers me, it's what he knows for sure that just ain't so."

So in 1983 Gail MacColl and I wrote *There He Goes Again: Ronald Reagan's Reign of Error,* a compilation of three hundred examples of dissembling and disinformation. Despite the book's careful documentation, it provoked an indignant response from Reagan loyalists and some journalists. Presidential aide David Gergen explained that because Reagan often spoke in parables ("like Lincoln"), errors on small details were less important than Reagan's "larger points." Then-commentator Pat Buchanan argued that other presidents misspoke more. Laurence Barrett of *Time*

"I'm going to run for president. I have all the qualifications. I'm on TV. I'm an actor. And I'm a liar."

(David Leisure, who plays Joe Isuzu on TV)

NEWS ITEM

"He once described to me how he got into politics by accident," says a former senior Administration official. **"He told me he told someone, 'By God, what am I doing in politics? The kinds of things I've done so far are far away from this. But then I thought that a substantial part of the political thing is acting and role playing and I know how to do that. So I used to worry, but I don't anymore.'"** (*New York Times,* 10/6/85)

thought our point was "exaggerated." And the President himself lampooned the book's line of criticism with his usual panache: during a campaign swing through New Jersey in October 1984, he actually said, "We must never again go back to the Carter-Mondale reign of error"!

With Reagan's landslide victory over Mondale, his systematic fibbing appeared to have been rewarded and, if anything, reinforced. Critics seemed destined to spend the rest of their lives driving their children over Ronald Reagan Highways to Ronald Reagan High Schools—while their kids would regard them as cranks on the subject of our revered 40th President.

Until Irangate.

What began as a Washington joke—"What did Reagan forget and when did he forget it?"—ended with him telling the Tower Commission, regarding his approval of arms shipments to Israel for Iran, "I just don't remember—period." Now that President Reagan has had to repudiate nearly everything he originally said about the Iranian arms sales, the public, by two-to-one in national surveys, believes he is lying. With that scandal, Mr. Teflon became Mr. Velcro.

This new sticky situation raises some unanswered questions: Is Reagan an average or excessive presidential prevaricator? Given the Niagara of evidence of Reagan's previous deceptions, why did it take six years for an acquiescing public and press to catch on? Will Reagan's revisionists succeed in isolating Irangate as an exception?

Public recognition of serious public deception in the Oval Office probably began with the U-2 spy-plane incident in 1960. President Eisenhower at first allowed his State Department to describe the vanished U-2 as a weather plane that strayed off course, until Gary Powers revealed the awkward truth. After the Cuban

Missile Crisis, State Department spokesman Arthur Sylvester created an uproar when he asserted that the government has a "right to lie" in urgent national-security situations. LBJ's lies about Vietnam and Nixon's about Watergate created a "credibility gap" that not unexpectedly soured Americans. By 1975, a national poll found that 69% of the public thought that "over the last ten years, this country's leaders have consistently lied to the people."

The post-Watergate era led to the disparate presidencies of Jimmy Carter and Ronald Reagan, who were as different as Jiminy Cricket and Pinocchio. Carter won the office in no small part because he wasn't the duplicitous Nixon, a perception reinforced by his perfectly pitched pledge, "I will never lie to you." There were, to be sure, small violations of this vow. In the classic TR-FDR-LBJ school of biographical puffing, Carter claimed to have been a "nuclear physicist" but wasn't. And press secretary Jody Powell, later citing a "troop movements" exception, misleadingly denied the administration had any rescue plans for the Iranian hostages right before the aborted Iranian rescue attempt. Still, however unpopular his presidency, there is a consensus that Jimmy Carter strove to tell the truth.

Not Ronald Reagan. He would shamelessly tell us that the Pope supported his policy of aiding the contras, that Justice Holmes remarked, "Keep government poor and remain free," that Brezhnev invented the idea of a nuclear freeze. None of these statements were true, nor were hundreds like them.

Indeed, he probably uttered more documented false statements at his initial November 19, 1986, press conference on the arms-for-hostages scandal than all the documented false statements of presidents Eisenhower, Kennedy, and Carter in their combined fifteen years in office. Among other evasions, recall that President Reagan denied

Israel's role in arms transfers, denied the arms sales were linked to the release of hostages, asserted all the weapons could easily fit into one plane, and argued his real goal was to end the Iran-Iraq war (by sending arms to the one side that refused to talk peace?).

These and other misstatements have led to some withering conclusions. Former Speaker Tip O'Neill has said that "he knows less than any president I've ever known." A joke making the rounds in Washington had Reagan defecting to the Soviets, only to be sent home because the Kremlin discovered that "he didn't know anything." The *Economist*'s verdict on Reagan's role in Irangate was, "Guilty, but asleep." A performer playing Reagan in the off-Broadway show *Rap Master Ronnie* said, "If you're right 90% of the time, why quibble over the remaining 3%?" And, yes, as Ralph Nader put it, he is probably our first president to own more horses than books.

Given the sudden new consensus on Reagan, it's fair to wonder why for so long "we licensed his beguiling forgeries," in the words of Garry Wills, author of *Reagan's America: Innocents at Home*. Perhaps the public was weary of so many failed presidents in a row. After Carter, the chief executive who always seemed to find the cloud, it was ready for a silver-lining leader. "I think we underestimate how much Americans want their president to be presidential," said scholar Richard Neustadt. "People are still hungry for a king. . . . It wasn't the legislative achievements of the first New Deal that established Roosevelt; it was the psychological turn-around. And Reagan is very Rooseveltian in this sense."

Reagan certainly played the part. He had, as Wills put it, the actor's "choreography of candor." " 'Well'—eyes down, eyes up, smile, slight dip of head to the right, and begin." Many enjoyed Reagan's rehearsed sincerity for the same reason they applaud another profession that elevates image over substance—magicians. "The public," said a spokesman for the Magicians' Association, "wants a fraud it can believe in."

It's one thing, however, for an instinctively trusting public to be swayed by a politician. But the press corps, too?

True, there were periodic articles about Reagan's "gaffes" or "mistakes." Essentially, though, the media before November 1986 had glorified Reagan. Why?

First, many journalists were mesmerized by the aura of the presidency in general, and Reagan's earlier stratospheric poll ratings in particular. Because Reagan was more popular than the press, concluded Robert Parry of *Newsweek,* the press "seemed to be a little fearful that if it wrote stories that were perceived as tough on this president, the public would not like them." Second, Reagan's charming reaction to and recovery from the 1981 assassination attempt gave him added insulation. Soon after, Roger Mudd reported that "most Americans want to give him a chance, and especially they want the media to give him a chance." Third, to expose Reagan surely meant risking loss of access to him and to those top aides on whom White House reporters relied for their information, a dependency that constrains every press corps assigned to a particular institution.

There were other constraints. Repeatedly saying the President was wrong would not be new, hence not news; so the administration could continue its routine fibs, knowing that the media wouldn't keep routinely exposing them. Also, because some journalists thought that chronicling Reagan's mistakes might have appeared partisan, they surrendered to a false objectivity: neutrality, then, meant covering neither Ronald Reagan's nor Walter Mondale's misstatements in 1984, even though only the former routinely made them.

“Let me suggest one thing. Don't let me get away with it. Check me out, but check everybody else out. Don't just take it for granted because you read it someplace or because someone stood up in a lecture course and told you from a lecture platform. You are the brightest and the best and make sure that you are hearing the facts, not just somebody's opinions.”
(9/9/85)

NEWS ITEM

Despite their longstanding friendship and similar political viewpoint, John Wayne wrote Reagan a blistering letter in 1977 telling him to stop spreading "untruths" about the Panama Canal Treaty. Wayne wrote: "I went to a lot of trouble and I brought in people to prove to you that most of the alarming things you are saying are untruths. . . . I'll show you point by God damn point in the treaty where you are misinforming people. This is not my point of view against your point of view. These are facts." (*New York Daily News,* 3/15/87)

Sidney Blumenthal, in a seminal *New Republic* piece, described another reason Reagan bested the media. "For Reagan, facts are means; for journalists, facts are ends." Since he only cared about symbols and universals (government is too big; the Soviets are evil), when the press occasionally cross-examined his "facts," Reagan couldn't have cared less.

Indeed, what he and his handlers really cared about was the *pictures* of his presidency. Martin Schram, in his book *The Great American Video Game,* describes how Reagan controlled the media by controlling their pictures of him. Schram notes how CBS correspondent Lesley Stahl once ran a long piece condemning the discrepancy between Reagan's photo opportunities and his programs. "Mr. Reagan," she said, "tries to counter the memory of an unpopular issue with a carefully chosen backdrop that actually contradicts the President's policy. Look at the handicapped Olympics, or the opening ceremony of an old-age home. No hint that he tried to cut the budget for the disabled and for federally subsidized housing for the elderly." Later, she was shocked when a Reagan aide phoned to thank her for the piece. "They [viewers] didn't hear what you are saying," he explained to Stahl, "if the pictures are saying something different."

And last, many in the media didn't pursue Reagan's misstatements because few of them wanted to believe that the leader of the free world was either a chronic liar or an amiable dunce.

The Reagan White House grew contemptuous of the compliant media. When shown that Reagan had "cited" a nonexistent British law in order to disparage gun control, for example, press secretary Larry Speakes responded, "It made the point, didn't it?" George Bush's press secretary laughed off misstatements made during televised debates, because "if reporters document that a candidate spoke untruthfully, so what? Maybe two hundred people read it."

Then-chief-of-staff Donald Regan referred to himself with bravado last year as the "shovel brigade," i.e., cleaning up after the President's elephantine blunderings of Bitburg, Reykjavik, and the Libyan disinformation campaign.

Consistent with all this disdain was Reagan's unavailability to the media. While LBJ averaged a press conference every two weeks and presidents Ford and Carter averaged one every four weeks, Reagan has met the press only every eight weeks on the average.

The Iran debacle, though, has now performed like the little boy telling the naked truth about his overrated emperor. For Reagan's deceptions were so glaring and frequent as to overcome the media's presumption in favor of a sitting president, especially such a popular one. After all, this President had repeatedly pledged as a first principle that he'd never encourage terrorism by trading arms for hostages; and the month before selling Iran arms, he had called that country an example of an "outlaw state run by the strangest collection of misfits, looney tunes, and squalid criminals since the advent of the Third Reich."

Here was the equivalent of an Elmer Gantry caught in bed, or with his hand in the till. It was a hypocrisy so obvious that Reagan's usual evasions, denials, and head bobs couldn't cut any ice. And when his popularity suffered an unprecedented plunge—one of every three Reagan supporters jumped ship in November–December 1986—the media plunged in.

Journalists David Wise and Anthony Marro trace presidential deception generally to the proliferation of Cold War covert operations. These required cover stories which, in turn, required government-sanctioned lies—from the U-2 incident to the bombing of Cambodia to Irangate. And once presidents got into the habit of dissembling

"You'd be surprised how much [being] a good actor pays off." (*Wash. Post,* 5/7/84)

NEWS ITEM

"What do you do when your president ignores all the palpable, relevant facts and wanders in circles? I could not bear to watch this good and decent man go on in this embarrassing way. I buried my head in my plate." (*The Triumph of Politics* by David Stockman)

for reasons of national security about operations abroad, it was a short next step to stretch national security to include embarrassments at home.

Considering this President, there are three favored interpretations for all his misstatements: habit, ignorance, and deceit.

As for habit, remember that he spent his formative years as a sportscaster inventing color commentary from a wire-service ticker and as an actor reading a script. What counted was effect, not accuracy, a habit he apparently cannot unlearn.

Political-science professor James David Barber, author of *The Presidential Character,* describes this school of thought:

Long before Reagan became a professional actor, he was trained in pretending. As a young boy he was extremely nearsighted and had to bluff his way through lessons in school because he couldn't see the blackboard. More pretending was necessary to hush up and conjure away from reality his father Jack's drinking. He got his first radio job as a sports announcer in an era when live broadcasts were faked by embellishing reports coming over the telegraph. The few facts set a framework and the rules of the game, a boundary within which he could spin fantasized variations. Given Reagan's flair for the dramatic, it became quite natural for him to begin making up stories about himself—little mythlets he seems to believe.

Another explanation is innocence by reason of ignorance. He wasn't aware of the diversion of money to the contras, explained Attorney General Meese, "because we didn't tell him." The tactic of "plausible deniability" is very plausible with a person so widely ridiculed for overreliance on 3×5 cards and with jokes about getting up at the crack of noon. ("Reagan Intellect Surprises Some," read a classic headline in 1984 in the *Wall Street Journal*.) Reagan is unusually uninformed for a president not only because of his own lack of intellectual curiosity, but also due to staff reinforcement. "He wouldn't get asked things that he wouldn't agree with," said Frederick N. Khedouri, a former top aide to Vice-President George Bush. "There was a kind of self-control or self-censorship by the staff. People wouldn't bring him something if they knew he would be averse to it." (Robert McFarlane told the Iran-Contra congressional hearing that he didn't have "the guts" to tell President Reagan his real opinion of US policy to Nicaragua because other cabinet-level officials "would have said I was some kind of commie.")

The third school of thought cites not ignorance but deception, for Reagan often elevates ideology over evidence. Thus, errors appear to be the result of not only ignorance but also strategy. Sure, all presidents err, just as all check-out clerks can ring the cash register wrong. But if a clerk *over*charged you ten times in a row, you would begin to suspect fraud rather than accident. So, too, with Reagan's errors, which also always favor the house—the White House. So if a good anecdote advances a right-wing cause, he won't let the facts get in his way. Does he realize the irony of using deception to defeat Soviet disinformation? Humorist Calvin Trillin describes the method in his book *With All Disrespect: More Uncivil Liberties*: "If a cherry tree in the White House Rose Garden got chopped down and all the evidence pointed to Ronald Reagan, he would say, 'I cannot tell a lie; there's a lady in California who picks up her welfare check every week in a Cadillac.'"

 t is this powerful combination of personal and ideological habits that makes Reagan so incorrigible. He is simply incapable of entertaining information that conflicts with his ideology. When facts differ from his beliefs, he

TALL TALE

At the 1985 National Prayer Breakfast, Reagan told a story about "an Asian monk" who charged into the Roman Coliseum, made his way into the arena, and shouted at the gladiators, "In the name of Christ, stop!" Immediately, a gladiator "plunged a sword" into the monk, killing him. "Then a strange thing began to happen," Reagan added. "Way up in the upper tiers, a man stood and made his way to the exit. Others began to follow. In dead silence everyone left the Coliseum. And that was the last battle to the death between the gladiators." The real story, however, can be found in John Pearson's book *Arena*. "In the year 404," Pearson wrote, "the Coliseum was the scene of the bizarre event which was to mark the definitive end of the whole cult of the gladiators in Rome. Telemachus, a monk from Asia Minor,

changes the facts, not his beliefs. He has sunk to a point where he can't make a major statement without making a major misstatement. And since imitation is flattery, his methods have inspired a culture of misspeak throughout his administration. What were all the doctored chronologies and shredded truths of the Iran-Contra scandal but the inevitable result of loyalists playing follow-the-leader? As the *Washington Post* put it, the gang that couldn't shoot straight in Iran couldn't tell it straight in America.

Hence, this updated edition.

While some might regard such a sequel as "piling on," it's essential to chronicle Reagan's more recent "errors" for at least two audiences—the next generation of citizens and the next generation of candidates.

Citizens should not be misled by Reagan revisionists trying to explain away the Iran-Contra episode. Columnist William F. Buckley, Jr., acknowledges only that, yes, the President has slipped "on a banana peel"; radio commentator Barry Farber argues that Reagan's lies are merely "snowflakes in a blizzard"; Reed Irvine, the far-right media critic, blasts the "left-wing" press for excessive and biased coverage; and Pat Buchanan says that FDR, too, broke some laws. In other words, Reagan's misstatements are trivial and typical.

Only by accumulating the volume and pattern of his errors can we assure that revisionists don't succeed in prettifying Reagan any better than they perfumed Nixon. Reagan's Iran scandal should, to paraphrase Churchill, sound like a thirteenth chime of a clock, which raises questions about all that preceded and followed it. Who again believed the Great Oz after Toto pulled back the curtain?

Also, future candidates and presidents must be encouraged to emulate the FDR model, not the RR model. Both performed well on stage. But while Reagan reminds us of

Chauncey Gardiner of Jerzy Kosinski's novel *Being There*, Roosevelt stuck to the facts. His speechwriter Robert Sherwood observed, in *Roosevelt and Hopkins*:

The New York Times *can make mistakes—the* World Almanac *can make mistakes—but the President of the United States must not make mistakes. This constant thought imposed a harrowing responsibility. After 1940, the White House had its resident statistician, Isador Lubin, the Commissioner of Labor Statistics, who was constantly available and incalculably valuable to Roosevelt and to Hopkins in checking every decimal point.*

This kind of precision from the nation's chief executive and chief newsmaker is indispensable to effective government and a working democracy. If a president argues that tax cuts always increase revenues and that South African leaders oppose segregation, how can sound policies result? And if a president regularly dissembles, how can the public ever be confident when he *is* telling the truth? Sissela Bok, in her book *Lying: Moral Choices in Public and Private Life*, put the problem well:

Imagine a society, no matter how ideal in other respects, where word and gesture could never be counted upon. Questions asked, answers given, information exchanged—all would be worthless. A warning that a well was poisoned or a plea for help in an accident would come to be ignored unless independent confirmation could be found. . . . Trust is a social good just as much as the air we breathe or the water we drink.

Whatever the short-term gains of dissembling and disinformation, the best rule—for incumbents and all their heirs—is that you can't lead people by misleading them. It's a lesson that our 40th President still hasn't learned.

TALL TALE CONT.

rushed into the arena and . . . attempted to separate the gladiators. Not to be cheated of the sight of blood, the crowd tore him to pieces. [The Emperor] Honorius responded by abolishing the gladiators and their games forever." (*Newsday*, 2/1/85)

REAGAN GAFFE EARLY WARNING SYSTEM

Don't sit defenseless during news conferences, hoping against hope that he's got it right. Be able to tell when Ronald Reagan has just dropped a big one. Protect yourself and your family from all magnitude of incoming error. The Reagan Gaffe Early Warning System (R.G.E.W.S.) is an easy-to-use defensive weapon designed to withstand exaggeration and distortion launched by our 40th president, up to and including obscure federal budget calculations. Constructed of the most durable substance known to man—reason—R.G.E.W.S. is completely hardened to statistical blur, off-the-cuff anecdote, avuncular charm, and diverting rhetoric. *Installation is completely free.*

1. COMMON SENSE GAP. Exercise your skepticism. Please. If you find yourself saying, "Gee, that sounds funny to me," perk up—you're probably right. Reagan's potent biases lead to distortions that even a moderate amount of good sense can combat. Keep your own intuitive alarm system in good working order.

2. THE AUTHORITATIVE SOURCE. Any Reagan assertion that has sweep and authority is suspect. Such assertions often open with statements like, *"As history shows . . ."* or *"As a recent study/report/investigation shows. . . ."* Misleading information generally follows. A variation on this approach is the UNFAMILIAR QUOTATION: *"As FDR/JFK/Winston Churchill once said. . . ."* (They didn't.)

3. THE CASE HISTORY. The storyteller in Reagan loves to cite individual histories to explain general policy. The sentence will usually begin, *"I recently heard of a man who. . . ."* Case histories have a tendency to turn into TALL TALES.

4. THE CLINCHING DETAIL. Reagan relishes percentages, numbers with decimal points, statistics, dates. It all sounds so concrete. Would a president say 77.3% if it weren't correct? This one does, all the time.

5. THE FALSE FACT. *"For instance"* and *"as an example"* are Red Alerts—any information following these phrases must be questioned. The example given is likely to be a double threat—both wrong and unrepresentative. Reagan likes to universalize the aberrant—don't let him.

6. DENIAL. When you hear Reagan say at a news conference, *"Well, that just isn't so,"* in a tone of patient dismay, you can bet it *is* so.

7. REITERATION. *"As I have said many times . . . "* is one of Reagan's favorite verbal tags. Most of the time he really has said whatever he's about to say many times, in which case it has, through repetition, become hardened in error. But then again he may never have said it before in his life.

8. RHETORICAL QUESTIONS. When deserted by both fact and anecdote, Reagan will ask a rhetorical question. This question will pivot on what debators call "the planted axiom," a premise that is assumed to be true but is never actually discussed or defended.

9. THE DEMOCRATS. Reagan has been a standardbearer for the far right a lot longer than he's been a leader of all the people. Any time he explains his policy in terms of the mistakes the other party has made, be on the alert for major historical revisionism.

10. THE BIG WRAP-UP. In a conclusive and pre-emptive tone, Reagan often polishes off his argument with a definitive statement — a FUN FACT, perhaps—and it sounds like a cogent and biting summation of the issue. It's not.

THEY'RE ALL DIFFERENT COUNTRIES
Reagan & Foreign Policy

Ronald Reagan has never been much of an international globe-trotter. He has trouble remembering the names of other nations' leaders. He has only the sketchiest notion of other nations' histories. He likes to maintain a "Battle of the Super Powers" approach to foreign policy—that way he doesn't have to learn about other countries because they're only pawns in a larger struggle. Keep it simple, keep it clean. If a nation declares itself anti-Soviet it is, *de facto,* a "democracy." On the other hand, an insufficiently anti-Soviet foreign government is, *ipso facto,* "totalitarian" ("authoritarian" if it gets lucky and Jeane Kirkpatrick is feeling generous). There can be no end of praise for dictators in Argentina, in Korea, for Marcos in the Philippines and Pinochet in Chile—they are good men fighting the good fight. Human rights only complicate the issue. If Reagan could have it all his way, the world would be run as a high school color day: choose up sides, the blues against the reds; everybody has to play; only one side can win. Then we'd know how things stood, wouldn't we?

❝ *[Kissinger aide Sonnenfelt] has expressed the belief that in effect the captive nations [in Eastern Europe] should give up any claim of national sovereignty and simply become a part of the Soviet Union.* **❞** *(Time, 4/11/76)*

Time magazine's Washington correspondent Strobe Talbott reported that "nothing in any version of Sonnenfelt's remarks justified Reagan's charge."

WISHFUL THINKING DEPT. ➤

❝ *[The Canal Zone] is every bit as much American soil as is the land in the states that were carved out of the Gadsden and*

Louisiana purchases, as is the state of Alaska. 🎔 (*New Republic,* 4/17/76)

No, it's not. The Canal Zone was never US territory; its citizens were not automatically citizens of the US, as are the citizens of, say, Alaska. The US, in its 1903 treaty with Panama, was given the image of sovereignty, the right to behave as "if it were the sovereign," but never legal sovereignty. The US Supreme Court made reference to this in its *Vermilya-Brown Co.* v. *Connell* decision (1948): "Admittedly, Panama is territory over which we do not have sovereignty."

❝ *Arriving in Warsaw in 1977 President Carter got off the plane to announce to a startled satrap who rules that country on behalf of the Soviet Union, 'Our concept of human rights is preserved in Poland.'* 🎔 (*Wash. Post,* 2/4/80)

A staple of Reagan's basic campaign speech. Simply put, Carter never said any such thing.

❝ *There has been an attempt to harass those who are sympathetic with freeing Cuba.* 🎔 (*Wash. Post,* 3/10/80)

When pressed for specific cases of such harassment, Reagan stated that he had "no examples." As one reporter persisted, Reagan claimed, "I've got to keep moving," and left the room. His assertion left advisers as well as journalists nonplussed.

❝ *I remember when Hitler was arming and had built himself up—no one has created quite the military that the Soviet Union has, but comparatively he was in that way. Franklin Delano Roosevelt made a speech in Chicago. . . . In that speech, he called on the free world to quarantine Nazi Germany, to stop all communication, all trade, all relations with them until they gave up that militaristic course and agreed to join with the free*

WHAT A DIFFERENCE A DAY MAKES

1/7/80:

"I just don't believe the farmer should be made to pay a special price for our diplomacy, and I'm opposed to [the Soviet grain embargo]." (*Wash. Post,* 1/8/80)

1/8/80:

"If we are going to do such a thing to the Soviet Union as a full grain embargo, which I support, first we have to be sure our own allies would join us on this." (*Claremont* [NH] *Eagle Times,* 1/9/80)

◄ UNFAMILIAR QUOTATION

In December 1982, after a meeting with Guatemalan military ruler General Efrain Rios Montt, President Reagan said that Montt was getting a "bum rap," and was "totally dedicated to democracy." But Montt (who proudly told the President, "We have no scorched earth policy—we have a policy of scorched Communists") had already announced in August 1982 a state of siege so the government could, he said, "kill people legally."

According to Amnesty International, Montt's government has practiced "widespread killing, including extrajudicial execution of large numbers of rural noncombatants, including entire families as well as persons suspected of sympathy with violent or nonviolent opposition groups."

nations of the world in a search for peace . . . but the funny thing was he was attacked . . . for having said such a thing. Can we honestly look back and say that World War II would have taken place if we had done what he wanted us to do back in 1938? ” (3/3/81)

Try 1937. And can we honestly put words in FDR's mouth? Nowhere in FDR's "Quarantine Speech" did he refer to Hitler or Nazi Germany, nor did he appeal to the "free world" to isolate Germany. FDR was probably referring to imperial Japan, which had just renewed its attack on Nationalist China. Finally, FDR was not "attacked for having said such a thing"—the public response to the speech was largely favorable.

❝ *We think that we are helping the forces that are supporting human rights in El Salvador.* ❞ (3/6/81)

Think again. Twelve thousand people were killed in El Salvador in 1980. According to Amnesty International, the "majority" of those murders were committed by the military, and it is the military regime that the US is "helping" in El Salvador.

❝ *Can we abandon this country [South Africa] that has stood beside us in every war we've ever fought?* ❞ (*New Republic*, 5/2/81)

Perhaps the President would find abandonment of South Africa and its apartheid policies easier if he knew that the Afrikaners, South Africa's current ruling party, *opposed* South Africa's entry into both world wars but were overruled by the then-governing pro-British majority. In fact, every South African prime minister since 1948, except one, was imprisoned during World War II for pro-Nazi sympathies.

PROS & CONS:

The Olympic Boycott

How can we condone putting the Olympics in Moscow? . . . I support the idea of taking the Olympics someplace else. (*Lansing* [MI] *Journal*, 2/14/80)

I favored the boycott, but since we are going to be the only ones I find myself worrying about the young people who trained so long. I don't like withholding visas. Leave it to the athletes. (March 31, *New York Times*, 4/6/80)

The government was not withholding visas and did not threaten to do so.

If just one country doesn't show up, I think the Soviet propaganda machine probably grinds out something like the United States didn't come because they were afraid of getting beaten. (*Wash. Post*, 4/1/80)

At least 25 other governments supported Carter's appeal for the boycott.

We should boycott the Moscow Olympics. I think our allies should, too. (April 4, *New York Times*, 4/6/80)

I just cannot within myself now find it right that the President of the United States should now be able to say to Americans who have violated no laws or anything, that they cannot go and cannot leave this country. (*New York Times*, 4/9/80)

I support the boycott today, I supported it yesterday. And I supported it when the President first called for it. (*New York Times*, 4/11/80)

The boycott was always voluntary—the United States Olympic Committee voted to support Carter's appeal and urged its athletes not to attend the Summer Games in Moscow.

China Syndromes

I n mid-August 1980, George Bush was dispatched to the Far East to prove that Reagan had a coherent foreign policy for that part of the world. This arrival of the Republican team upon the international scene was less than entirely successful. In fact, Ronald Reagan's comments—such as referring to Taiwan as the "free Republic of China"—seemed designed to spoil his running mate's stay in Peking. (Source for all quotes: *The New York Times* August 20, 24, 25, 26, 1980.)

This "liaison" would violate the Taiwan Relations Act of 1979, ruling out official government relations between the US and Taiwan.

5/17

REAGAN:

"One of the things I look forward to most if I am successful in this election is to re-establish official relations between the United States government and Taiwan. . . . That liaison office [in Taiwan] is unofficial. It is not governmental. It is a private kind of thing. And I have said before that I see no reason why, with an embassy in Peking, we could not now have an official liaison office in Taiwan. . . ."

8/16

REAGAN:

Q: "Do you advocate a 'government to government relationship' with Taiwan?"

A: *"Yes, I think that liaison—this is what I stress—that could be official."*

8/16

BUSH:

"I will articulate as best I can the objectives of the Reagan foreign policy and they will be refreshingly received in Peking, I can assure you."

8/19

BUSH:

"Governor Reagan hasn't proposed a two-Chinas policy, nor does he intend to propose such a policy. We don't advocate diplomatic relations with Taiwan, nor have we."

8/22

REAGAN:

Q: *"Are you still for 'official relations' with Taiwan, yes or no?"*
A: *"Um, I guess it's a yes."*

8/23

PEKING:

"[Mr. Reagan's] remarks are absolutely not a slip of the tongue. He has insulted one billion Chinese people."

8/23

BUSH:

"No comment."

8/25

REAGAN:

"I don't know that I said that or not, ah, I really don't."

8/25

BUSH:

"He did not say that. If you're referring to the press conference I attended, the Governor did not say 'government to government relations.'"

8/25

REAGAN:

"I misstated."

NEWS ITEM

In an attempt to downgrade President Carter's initiative on US–China policy, President Reagan said, "In the first place, China relations had been normalized by the visits of a previous President to a previous administration [i.e., Richard Nixon]. And I am not at all sure that [Carter] added anything to what had already been accomplished." (*Wash. Post,* 5/5/83) Carter added, of course, what *Washington Post* columnist Philip Geyelin labeled "the hard part"—the 1979 "normalization" agreement that established full diplomatic relations between the two countries.

WISHFUL THINKING DEPT.

DEPT. OF RETRACTIONS

After Mr. Reagan said he stood behind a campaign statement that Jerusalem should remain united under Israeli sovereignty, the White House was forced to issue a clarification on American policy in order to head off an international misunderstanding.

Although confirming that he had been quoted correctly, the White House indicated that the President's statement was not an accurate expression of administration policy. That policy remains support for an undivided Jerusalem whose ultimate fate will be decided by negotiations on a peace plan for the region. (*New York Times*, 11/20/81)

❝ *I've had a lengthy communication from the Pope. He approves what we've done so far.* **❞** (1/19/82)

Reagan's communication from the Pope may have been lengthy, but as the Vatican hastened to point out, it did not involve approving Washington's sanctions against Moscow after the crackdown in Poland.

❝ *I said there was a flurry about land reform [in El Salvador]. I understand that that has turned around, that there are thousands of people who have been given deeds to their plots. . . .* **❞** (7/29/82)

As of January 1983, according to the administration's own figures, not even one thousand Salvadorans had been given final title to their land as a consequence of the government's land reform program.

❝ *We have never interfered in the internal government of a country and have no intention of doing so, never have had any thought of that kind.* **❞** (9/28/82)

Never? That's not what an article on the front page of the *New York Times* on December 4, 1982, said: "United States covert activities in Central America, which began a year ago with limited aims, have become the most ambitious paramilitary and political action operation mounted by the CIA in nearly a decade, according to intelligence officials." Nor is it what the President himself said half a year later: "Now, if they [House Committee members] want to tell us that we can give money and do the same things we've been doing—money giving, providing subsistence, and so forth to these people [anti-Sandinista guerrillas] and making it overt instead of covert—that's all right with me." (*Wash. Post,* 5/5/83)

> *Well, I am pleased to announce today that the industrialized democracies have this morning reached substantial agreement to a plan of action. The understanding we've reached demonstrates that the Western alliance is fundamentally united. . . .*
> (Radio speech, 11/13/82)

Had France and England suddenly been stricken from the list of industrialized democracies? After Reagan made this announcement lifting pipeline sanctions against the USSR, British Foreign Minister Pym said that the European governments had made "no concessions" in return for what he said had been "a unilateral decision by the Americans." And France flatly contradicted the President's statement, asserting that it was "not a party to the agreement announced this afternoon in Washington."

> *We are not trying to do anything to try and overthrow the Nicaraguan government.* (4/14/83)

Consistent with the Boland Amendment, which prohibits the US from trying to overthrow the Nicaraguan government, the President maintained throughout early 1983 that US aid to anti-Sandinista guerrillas who *are* trying to overthrow that government was only an effort to persuade Nicaragua to stop shipping arms to El Salvador. Then, in an interview with reporters in May, President Reagan four times characterized those anti-Sandinista guerrillas as "freedom fighters"—a term he has not yet used to designate guerrillas in El Salvador. According to *Newsweek,* "Red-faced White House staff men did their best to dampen speculation that Reagan had been deceitful—or simply disengaged—by stressing that he was speaking from the heart." Which, no doubt, he was.

> *Our purpose, in conformity with American and interna-*

NEWS ITEM

Speaking in June 1982 the President described Syrian missiles in Lebanon as "offensive weapons," adding, "There's no question about the direction in which they're aimed." Well, naturally, there is *some* question, since the weapons under discussion are surface-to-air missiles used for anti-aircraft purposes—they are, therefore, aimed in the direction of whatever is flying over them and are entirely *defensive* in nature. (*Wash. Post,* 6/17/82)

66 I remember a happier time when there was a tradition that the President of the US never left our shores, but I don't say that you could do that today. 99
(*Time*, 11/17/80)

A LESSON FROM HISTORY ▶

tional law, is to prevent the flow of arms to El Salvador, Honduras, Guatemala, and Costa Rica. 99 (4/27/83)

Such a purpose does not conform to law, at least not according to one hundred law professors from all over the United States who, in a statement last year, declared that the administration's plan to covertly destabilize the government of Nicaragua constituted a serious violation of both international and domestic law. They stated that the charter of the Organization of American States prohibits "covert destabilization of any O.A.S. member state." Article 15 of the charter provides: "No state or group of states has the right to intervene, directly or indirectly, for any reason whatever, in the internal or external affairs of any other state. The foregoing principle prohibits not only armed force but also any other form of interference or attempted threat against the personality of the state or against its political, economic, and cultural elements."

66 If you remember, the Organization of American States asked Somoza to resign at that time. And Somoza, his reply to them was that if it would benefit his country, Nicaragua, he would. And he did resign. 99 (5/4/83)

Somoza did officially resign from office, but only under threat of his life. By July 17, 1979, the morning Somoza fled to Miami, the Sandinistas had already set up an interim government at Leon, Nicaragua; had surrounded Managua, the capital of Nicaragua, on all sides; and were rapidly closing in on the city. Possibly the next day, and no later than July 19, the Sandinistas occupied Managua and the National Guard disbanded. So Somoza "resigned," not because it would "benefit" his country, or because the OAS had asked him to do so eight months previously, but because he wanted to save himself. The man Somoza chose to succeed him as president lasted in office no more than 30 hours.

" But we are the ones who have gone a step beyond that [Camp David agreement] with regard to trying to have an overall peace in the entire area. That had never been proposed. " (5/4/83)

According to columnist Philip Geyelin writing in the *Washington Post*, overall peace "has been proposed in the so-called Rogers plan under Nixon and regularly by Henry Kissinger; it is the bedrock of the Camp David Accords." Indeed, the preamble to the Accords states: "The parties are determined to reach a just, comprehensive, and durable settlement of the Middle East conflict."

" Well, I learned a lot. . . . I went down [to Latin America] to find out from them and [learn] their views. You'd be surprised. They're all individual countries. " (Wash. Post, 12/6/82)

Vietnam, A Noble Cause

Maybe the reason Ronald Reagan thinks the Vietnam War was "a noble cause," thinks it was "a war which our government refused to win," thinks there is "no parallel between Vietnam and El Salvador," is that he really doesn't know much about it. Or, to put it another way, what he thinks he knows is mostly wrong. Two lengthy renditions of the History of the Vietnam War According to Ronald Reagan have been made available by their originator—in a January 1978 radio speech and a February 18, 1982 presidential press conference. Both are sadly garbled.

❝ *There were two Vietnams, north and south. They had been separate nations for centuries.* **❞** (Radio, Jan. 1978)

When not artificially divided by the Chinese or French colonialists, Vietnam was politically united for much of its history.

❝ *Both became colonial possessions of France in what was known as French Indo-China and both were freed a few years after World War II as one after another of the European colonial empires were liquidated.* **❞** (Radio, Jan. 1978)

Under French colonization, Vietnam was divided into three administrative units: Cochin China, Annam, and Tonkin. In 1950, these three sections were unified by the French under Emperor Bao Dai. The French did not "free" any part of Vietnam. It was taken from them by Vietnamese anti-colonial forces during a long and bitter conflict that culminated in the battle of Dien Bien Phu, where the French were handed a decisive loss. President Eisenhower turned down a French request for American bombing support at Dien Bien Phu, although by that time the US was bankrolling the French effort.

This battle took place in the spring of 1954, nearly a decade— not "a few years"—after WW II.

❝ Vietnam returned to its pre-colonial status as two nations. The great powers in Geneva set down a plan, first, to allow the people of both countries to move to whichever of the two they chose without interference, and second, for an internationally supervised election by the people as to whether they wanted to unite or continue as separate nations. ❞ (Radio, Jan. 1978)

The first sentence is meaningless, as Vietnam did not have pre-colonial status as two nations. As for the great powers in Geneva, the Geneva Conference of 1954 set up a *temporary* partition of Vietnam at the 17th parallel and called for *national* elections to be held two years later. The brand-new government of South Vietnam refused to sign the Geneva accords or to participate in elections, which were never held. The accords did not stipulate a ballot question on uniting or separating for the simple reason that they treated Vietnam as a single country, making no mention of two separate states. The US would not give even oral consent to the Final Declaration of Geneva, the part containing a call for free general elections.

❝ The Communist dictator of North Vietnam, Ho Chi Minh, refused to hold the elections and when a million of his people started moving south away from communism (under the terms of the agreement) his troops barricaded the frontier and halted the migration. ❞ (Radio, Jan. 1978)

Once again, it was the newly created South, not the North, that refused to hold elections. In fact, Ho Chi Minh complained when balloting did not occur. President Eisenhower, in his memoirs, stated that experts agreed that "possibly 80% of

PROBLEM SOLVING

❝ We should declare war on North Vietnam . . . We could pave the whole country and put parking strips on it, and still be home by Christmas. ❞ (Fresno *Bee,* 10/10/65)

34

"Because Vietnam was not a declared war, the veterans are not even eligible for the G.I. Bill of Rights with respect to education or anything." (*Newsweek*, 4/21/80)

Sure they are. Even if Vietnam wasn't a declared war. Apparently Reagan's mind wandered during an earlier meeting with two high-ranking military officers who were trying to tell him that peacetime veterans of the all-volunteer army did not receive education benefits.

the population would have voted for the Communist Ho Chi Minh as their leader" if elections had been held. The armistice section of the Geneva accords provided a 300-day period of civilian movement across the demilitarized zone at the 17th parallel. During this period, the US Seventh Fleet helped some 860,000 people, mostly Catholics, move from the northern zone to the southern, where a devout Catholic named Diem was assuming control. Ho's troops didn't have to "barricade the frontier"—it was closed to civilian movement at the end of the 300-day period.

❝ *And openly, our country sent military advisers there to help a country which had been a colony have such things as a national security force, an army if you might say, or a military to defend itself. And they were doing this, I recall correctly, also in civilian clothes, no weapons, until they began being blown up where they lived in walking down the street by people riding by on bicycles and throwing pipe bombs at them, and then they were permitted to carry sidearms or wear uniforms. . . .* **❞** (2/18/82)

The United States Military Assistance Advisory Group, in uniforms, with weapons, arrived in South Vietnam in the late '50s to create and train a South Vietnamese army. By the early '60s, as insurgency grew and the troubled Diem regime crumbled, "combat support"—in the form of what was, by 1963, 16,000 American soldiers ("advisers")—was supplied to the army of the Republic of South Vietnam. To suggest that uniforms and weapons were withheld from American troops in Vietnam until they were being blown up by pipe bombs thrown from bicycles is ludicrous.

66 . . . but . . . when these attacks and forays became so great, . . . John F. Kennedy authorized the sending in of a division of marines, and that was the first move toward combat moves in Vietnam. 99 (2/18/82)

In the face of a rapidly deteriorating military and political situation—of somewhat larger proportions than "attacks and forays" on individual American soldiers—the first official American ground troops were sent to Vietnam. They were in the form of two—not one—US Marine Corps divisions, and they landed at the US air base in Danang in March 1965—nearly a year and a half after JFK's assassination.

66 I have a feeling that we are doing better in the war than the people have been told. 99 (*L.A. Times*, 10/16/67)

FOCUS OF EVIL
Reagan & the USSR

When it comes to the Red army, the President puts his voice-in-the-wilderness pedal to the floor: he repeats his warning—they're bigger than we are, they're better than we are—even if he must stand alone. And alone he has stood, as administration figures and even Republicans hesitate to join him in awarding the #1 superpower slot to the USSR. (According to the Department of Defense's own Annual Report for fiscal 1982, "The United States and the Soviet Union are roughly equal in strategic nuclear power.") America doesn't need all that much convincing on the subject of the Soviet menace, so why the hyperbole? Sure they've been pursuing a defense build-up program, sure they've got new weapons, sure there's cause for concern, but as the Reagan rhetoric heats up, skepticism may be the only way to keep cool. And an America skeptical about huge increases in defense spending is not what Ronald Reagan has in mind.

FALSE ALARM ➤

Kissinger is quoted as saying that he thinks of the US as Athens and the Soviet Union as Sparta. [Kissinger says] 'the day of the US is past, and today is the day of the Soviet Union. . . . My job as Secretary of State is to negotiate the most acceptable second-best position available.' (TV speech, *New York Times*, 4/1/76)

Reagan did not cite sources. Kissinger, denying the remarks, said that as an historian he could not have made the Sparta-Athens analogy because "Athens outlasted Sparta by several centuries." Lawrence S. Eagleburger, a State Department counselor, called the remarks "pure invention and totally irresponsible." James Reston pointed out that the accusation originated with Admiral Elmo R. Zumwalt, Chief of Naval Operations (1970–74). According to Reston, Zumwalt was quoted in *Parade* magazine, "which had the decency to publish a flat denial that Mr. Kissinger had said anything of the sort. Mr. Reagan was not so fair."

❝ *As a matter of fact, where this [report on USSR military capability] came from is the defense expert of the Library of Congress. . . . He said for a time it was our qualitative advantage that kept us ahead in spite of their quantitative advantage. But he had to say that no longer is true.* **❞** (New Republic, 6/12/76)

The report said that our qualitative advantage was less than it used to be, but that we still had it. See below.

❝ *Sen. Clark, of Iowa, [stated] that he asked the military experts of the Library of Congress to give him a report and admitted that he wanted it because he believed that all this talk and all of the administration requests for more money was because they were just simply building a scarecrow to get more money for defense. And so he thought he would get a report from the Library of Congress that would bear this out and he had to admit himself that he got a report from the Library that was probably more terrifying than any of the statements I have made— the report that we were indeed in a very dangerous position.* **❞** (New Republic, 6/12/76)

Reagan made these comments in an interview with John Osborne, who then discovered that it was Sen. John C. Culver, not Sen. Dick Clark, who asked for the report from the Library of Congress. According to Culver's defense specialist, the Senator and his staff did not expect the report to say any particular thing; they were not "surprised" by what they got; the report concluded that the margin of US superiority was smaller but still there; Sen. Culver never got close to characterizing the report as "terrifying."

❝ *Let us be aware that while they [the Soviets] preach the supremacy of the state, declare its omnipotence over individual man, and predict its eventual domination of all peoples of the earth— they are the focus of evil in the modern world.* **❞** (3/8/83)

FALSE ALARM

"On balance, the Soviet Union does have a definite margin of superiority [in nuclear arms]." (3/31/82)

"I don't think there'd be much accomplishment in freezing the Soviet Union into a position of superiority over the rest of us." (6/1/82)

"The Soviet Union does have a decided edge on us [in nuclear forces]." (7/11/82)

"Unless we demonstrate the will to rebuild our strength and restore the military balance, the Soviets, since they are so far ahead, have little incentive to negotiate with us." (11/22/82)

General David C. Jones, former chairman of the Joint Chiefs of Staff, said that he would not swap the American defense establishment for the Soviet one. According to former Secretary of State

❝ . . . We are second in military strength to the Soviet Union. . . . The chief of engineering and research at the Pentagon, the top defense expert at the Library of Congress, the Secretary of the Army, and others have all stated and upheld this fact of where we are now in this second-best position. ❞ (New York Times, 6/27/76)

Each of the gentlemen mentioned had, on occasion, pointed to limited areas of Soviet military advantage. But the Ford administration and the Department of Defense maintained that there were also significant areas of American advantage, adding up to a "rough equivalence" over all.

❝ Up until now [the Soviet invasion of Afghanistan] the Soviet Union has not used its own military forces in its imperialism. It's taken over country after country, but it's done it with proxy troops. ❞ (Des Moines Register, 1/8/80)

Soviet troops were used in Hungary in 1956 and in Czechoslovakia in 1968.

❝ And so, in addition to their great military buildup, they [the Russians] have . . . practiced evacuation, when we finally began to learn the facts, we learned that in one summer alone, they took over 20 million young people out of the cities to the country to give them training in just living off the countryside. ❞ (Robert Scheer interview, Feb. 1980)

We? Nobody but Reagan seems to know about the Soviet evacuation of young people—the CIA says that there is no evidence the Russians have ever practiced evacuating their cities.

❝ Yes, they [the Russians] have gone very largely into a great civil defense program, providing shelters, some of their industry

is underground and all of it hardened to the point of being able to withstand a nuclear blast. **")** (Robert Scheer interview, Feb. 1980)

Scheer asserts in his book, *With Enough Shovels,* that he could find no expert who believed that all of Soviet industry is hardened to the point where it could withstand a nuclear blast. He also points out that the September 1978 CIA study of the Soviet civil defense program—the only complete CIA study of the subject—could find no evidence of hardened industry and that even those given to thinking the worst of the Russians could go no further than a belief that some industry is protected—and only against the indirect effects of a bomb.

") *Today, we are not equal to the Soviet Union, and that is why they were able to cross into Afghanistan.* **")** (*The New Yorker,* 3/24/80)

There must be other reasons—an unquestioned US military and nuclear superiority did not seem to deter Soviet troops from crossing into Hungary in 1956, or 12 years later into Czechoslovakia.

") *Now, the Soviets have 945 warheads aimed at targets in Europe in their medium-ranged missiles. And we have no deterrent whatsoever. . . .* **")** (10/14/82)

Hardly. The US now has, on submarines in both the Atlantic and the Mediterranean, 400 warheads targeted at the Soviet Union. Also on these subs are all additional 4,500 warheads not officially committed to NATO. Great Britain has 192 warheads targeted at the USSR; France has 98. The President is also ignoring the bomber forces of both the US and NATO, which have the capacity to drop well over 1,000 nuclear weapons on the USSR.

FALSE ALARM CONT.

Alexander Haig, "our systems are both more sophisticated and reliable and more technologically sound" than the Soviets. And Defense Secretary Caspar Weinberger reported to Congress that the US arms buildup was intended to "prevent the Soviet Union from *acquiring . . .* superiority"— not keeping it.

HUH???

40

NEWS ITEM

In a November 1982 address to the nation, Reagan asserted, "Today, in virtually every measure of military power, the Soviet Union enjoys a decided edge." One month later, during an interview with Independent Radio Network correspondents, he was asked, "Would you trade American forces for Soviet forces?" His reply: "No."

PROBLEM SOLVING

❝ Why shouldn't the Western world quarantine the Soviet Union until they decide to behave as a civilized nation?❞ (*New York Times*, 1/17/80)

❝ *Soviet leaders invest 12–14% of their country's GNP in military spending, two to three times the level we invest.* ❞ (11/22/82)

Misleading—our GNP is twice theirs. So the 6–7% of our GNP that we invest in military spending is roughly equal to their 12–14%. Besides, both the Pentagon and the CIA admit that they don't know how much the Soviets spend on defense. However, the Pentagon does estimate that in the past decade, according to the prestigious Institute for Strategic Studies, the US and its NATO allies outspent the USSR and its Warsaw Pact allies by $300 billion.

❝ *The Soviet Union put to sea 60 new ballistic missile submarines in the last 15 years. Until last year we had not commissioned one in that same period.* ❞ (11/22/82)

According to the *New York Times* (11/24/82), there is virtually unanimous expert judgment that American submarines, despite their age, remain decidedly superior in overall performance.

❝ *The Soviet Union has built over 200 modern Backfire bombers—and is building 30 more a year. For 20 years, the US has deployed no new strategic bombers.* ❞ (11/22/82)

Again, prevailing military judgment in the US Air Force is that the B-52, despite age, is a better long-range bomber than the Backfire.

❝ *The Soviet Union has deployed a third more land-based intercontinental ballistic missiles than we have. Believe it or not, we froze our number in 1965 and have deployed no additional missiles since then.* ❞ (11/22/82)

We don't believe it. While the *number* of missiles hasn't changed since 1967—not 1965—the *quality* has. Minute Man IIs and IIIs have replaced the original Is. In addition, every administration, beginning with Richard Nixon's, has chosen to increase the number of nuclear warheads on each missile, rather than the number of missiles, a choice experts say was deliberately made for strategic reasons.

❝ *This is what they [the Russians] said of themselves. That they reserved these rights to break a promise, to change their ways, to be dishonest, and so forth if it furthered the cause of socialism. Now, just the other day, one among you [journalists] somewhere has written and commented on that and has quoted the ten commandments of Nikolai Lenin . . . the ten principles—guiding principles of communism. And they're all there. That promises are like pie crusts, made to be broken. . . .* **❞** (1/20/83)

Lenin did make the pie crust reference, but he used it as a criticism of the conduct of his political opponents, not as a justification for his own actions. Discussing political infighting, Lenin wrote: "The promises, like pie crust, are leaven to be broken, says the English proverb." The search for the "Ten Commandments of Communism" continues.

❝ *Certainly their [the Soviet Union's] entire beliefs—beginning with the disbelief in God—their entire beliefs are so contrary to what we accept as morality. Witness a Kampuchea and an Afghanistan and so forth.* **❞** (3/18/83)

Morality and politics don't always mix. Witness the fact that it is the United States, not the Soviet Union, that recognizes Pol Pot's Khmer Rouge as the legitimate government of Kampuchea. It was under Pol Pot's reign, from 1975 to 1979, that an estimated three million Cambodians were massacred.

TEMPTATION OF PRIDE
Reagan & Defense/ Disarmament

More tanks. More bombers. More carriers and destroyers. Reagan wants so much more of everything that explodes that his own Republicans are getting jittery. Even John Connally and William Simon want him to slow down. As for arms control, the President never liked the idea of fewer nuclear weapons in the arsenal. After all, his opponents on the issue are dupes of Soviet propaganda. His source? *Reader's Digest,* probably (the FBI has been of no help at all). When you look at the buildup, never underestimate the power of Reagan's anti-Communist paranoia. Behind it all lies an absolute belief in Soviet military superiority. Haven't we heard this one before? Remember the bomber gap, the missile gap, and the ABM gap? The President does. And he's nostalgic for them, even though they never existed. Do you also remember the recent CIA discovery that the Soviets' real defense growth was not the 4% assumed but actually closer to 2%? You might as well forget it. The President already has.

UNFAMILIAR QUOTATION ➤

   " *Secretary of State Kissinger has expressed the view that you and I, the American people, lack the will and the stamina to do what is necessary to keep this country #1.* **"** (*New York Times,* 6/27/76)

Kissinger repeatedly disavowed any such statement. Reagan never backed it up with evidence, nor did he stop saying it.

   " *I am not talking of scrapping. I am talking of taking the [SALT II] treaty back, and going back into negotiations.* **"** (Presidential debate, 10/28/80)

Reagan had been virulently anti-SALT II for some time,

although he softened his position as the election approached. Some sample comments: "Send it back to the Soviets so fast they'll think we've got a new postal service"; "SALT II—ship that thing back to the Soviets in Moscow." Or from January 1980: "I've flatly called for shelving the SALT II treaty."

66 *Besides which, it [SALT II] is illegal, because the law of the land, passed by Congress, says that we cannot accept a treaty in which we are not equal.* 99 (Presidential debate, 10/28/80)

Whether or not the SALT II treaty was a good idea, it did not explicitly establish the US as being unequal to the USSR. Even if it had, it would still be legal if ratified by the US Senate.

66 *We then went back into negotiations on their [the Soviets'] terms, because Mr. Carter had cancelled the B-1 bomber, delayed the MX, delayed the Trident submarine, delayed the Cruise missile, shut down the . . . Minute Man missile production line. . . .* 99 (Presidential debate, 10/28/80)

The B-1 bomber had been delayed. As for the rest: the Cruise missile and MX were under full-scale development; the Minute Man missile's production line had been shut down because the production schedule had been met; and the first Trident submarine, the USS *Ohio*, had been launched on April 7, 1979.

66 *. . . I would like to correct a misstatement of fact by the President. I have never made the statement [that nuclear proliferation is 'none of our business'] about nuclear proliferation, and nuclear proliferation, or the trying to halt it, would be a major part of a foreign policy of mine.* 99 (Presidential debate, 10/28/80)

66 *So in your discussions of the nuclear freeze proposals, I urge you to beware the temptation of pride—the temptation blithely to declare yourselves above it all and label both sides equally at fault, to ignore the facts of history and the aggressive impulses of an evil empire, to simply call the arms race a giant misunderstanding and thereby remove yourself from the struggle between right and wrong, good and evil.* 99 (3/8/83)

◀ **UNFAMILIAR QUOTATION**

44

HUH???

Q: "Do you think there could be a battlefield exchange without having buttons pressed all the way up the line?"

A: "Well, I would—if they realized that we—if we went back to that stalemate, only because our retaliatory power, our seconds, or our strike at them after their first strike would be so destructive that they couldn't afford it, that would hold them off." (10/17/81)

66 *We're in greater danger today than we were the day after Pearl Harbor. Our military is absolutely incapable of defending this country.* 99 (*New York Times,* 4/12/80)

Jacksonville, Florida, January 31, 1980: "I just don't think it's any of our business. All of us would like to see non-proliferation—but I don't think we are succeeding. We're the only ones in the world that's trying to stop it." (*New York Times,* 2/1/80)

66 *But I do believe this: that it is rather foolish to have unilaterally disarmed, you might say, as we did. . . .* 99 (3/3/81)

The United States did not disarm in the '70s; it dramatically strengthened its nuclear forces. Some of the programs: (1970–75) Replacement of Minute Man I and II ICBMs with 550 Minute Man IIIs; (1970–76) MIRVing of 550 Minute Man III ICBMs; (1971–76) Replacement of Polaris A3 SLBMs with 496 Poseidon C-3 SLBMs; (1971–76) Addition of 65 FB-111 SAC bombers and 356 F-111 nuclear-capable bombers; (1971–77) MIRVing of 496 SLBMs on Poseidons; (1972–75) Addition of 1,140 short-range attack missiles to B-52 and FB-111 bombers; (1979–83) Retrofitting of 900 MK12A warheads on 300 Minute Man IIIs; (1979–82) Retrofitting of 192 Trident I missiles on 12 Poseidon submarines; (1976) Initiation of Trident submarine program; (1981) Air-launched Cruise Missile operational; the first of at least 4,350 to go on B-52s; (1970s) B-52 and FB-111 improvements—20 programs; (1970s) ICBM improvements—5 programs. In 1970, the United States had 4,000 strategic nuclear warheads. By the end of the decade, it had almost 10,000.

66 *There is one area, however, where we must spend more and that is for our national defense. Now don't get me wrong. Cap Weinberger . . . has shown me programs in his department where we can and will realize substantial savings. We'll cut*

$2.9 billion in next year's budget alone, and the cuts will accumulate to more than $28 billion by 1986 in the Defense Department. **"** (3/30/81)

Twenty-eight billion dollars over five years is approximately 2% of the defense budget—as compared to a nearly 100% increase in that proposed budget over the same period from $182.9 billion in 1982 to $377 billion in 1988.

" *I do have to point out that everything that has been said and everything in their [Soviet defense] manuals indicates that, unlike us, the Soviet Union believes that a nuclear war is possible. And they believe it's winnable. . . .* **"** (10/17/81)

Not unlike us. The US Army field manual *Nuclear, Biological and Chemical Reconnaissance and Decontamination Operations* from February 1980 says, "The US Army must be prepared to fight and win when nuclear weapons are used." Senior adviser to the National Security Council (1981–82) Richard Pipes' views were summarized in the *Washington Post* as follows: "His strategy, which he says reflects official thinking, is a winnable nuclear war." And the US budget for Fiscal Year 1983 states, "US defense policies ensure our preparedness to respond to and, if necessary, successfully fight either conventional or nuclear war."

" *During the last 10 years, the United States decreased its military spending.* **"** (1/14/82)

" *As you can see . . . in constant dollars, our defense spending in the 1960s went up because of Vietnam. And then it went downward through much of the 1970s.* **"** (11/22/82)

Not so. According to the controller of the Department of Defense, the US defense budget, in 1982 constant dollars,

LITTLE KNOWN FUN FACT

" *I recently learned something quite interesting about video games. Many young people have developed incredible hand, eye, and brain coordination in playing those games. The air force believes these kids will be our outstanding pilots should they fly our jets.* **"** (3/8/83)

66 I could see where you could have the exchange of tactical [nuclear] weapons against troops in the field without it bringing either one of the major powers to pushing the button.99 (10/17/81)

WISHFUL THINKING DEPT. ➤

was *$179.9 billion* in 1971, while we were fighting a war with Vietnam; in 1981, that constant dollar figure was *$193.9* billion.

66 *The leader of Ground Zero does not believe in the freeze. A freeze, yes, but after, as we've said so many times, a verifiable, substantial reduction to bring us down to parity and at a reduced number.* 99 (4/20/82)

Roger Molander, the head of Ground Zero, said that "the President really misrepresents my position on the freeze." Though he has not taken a position on the freeze proposal, Molander disagrees with Reagan's view that the Soviet Union possesses nuclear superiority over the United States.

66 *Those [nuclear weapons] that are carried in ships of one kind or another, or submersibles, you are dealing there with a conventional type of weapon or instrument, and those instruments can be intercepted. They can be recalled.* 99 (5/13/82)

Submarine-launched missiles cannot be recalled. If the President thinks differently he may be surprised in a nuclear exchange.

66 *What we're striving for is to reduce the power, the number, and particularly those destabilizing missiles that can be touched off by the push of a button.* 99 (5/13/82)

The destabilizing impact of land-based ICBMs is not that they can be touched off by the push of a button. They can't be. They destabilize the balance between American and Soviet nuclear forces because their great accuracy might encourage a preemptive nuclear first strike. Nevertheless, this administration has gone ahead with the two most accurate and destabilizing missiles ever built—MX and Trident II.

" *There is no question about foreign agents that were sent to help instigate and help create and keep such a movement [the nuclear freeze movement] going.* **"** (11/11/82)

Reagan's comments refer to the huge anti-nuclear rally—almost one million people—held in New York's Central Park on June 12, 1982. Edward J. O'Malley, assistant director of intelligence for the FBI, told the House Select Committee that fall that he "would not attribute the large turnout" to Soviet agents. Rep. Edward Boland, chairman of the committee, said his panel's hearings led to the conclusion that "Soviet agents have had no significant influence in the nuclear freeze movement."

" *Incidentally, the first man who proposed the nuclear freeze was in February 21st, 1981, in Moscow—Leonid Brezhnev.* **"** (12/10/82)

Nope. The freeze idea was first officially proposed by Sen. Mark Hatfield (R-Ore.), in 1979, as an amendment to SALT II.

" *You have to remember, we don't have the military industrial complex that we once had, when President Eisenhower spoke about it.* **"** (1/5/83)

What we do have is the military industrial complex Eisenhower was trying to warn us against. In that famous farewell address, Ike said, "We must guard against the acquisition of unwarranted influence . . . by the military industrial complex. The potential for the disastrous rise of misplaced power exists and will persist."

" *I was the one who took the lead to begin bringing about the first real arms reduction talks that we've ever been able to hold with the Soviet Union. . . .* **"** (2/16/83)

" *You start with the fact that the government has a sizable layer of fat, no matter how worthwhile the program. And I would include defense in that.* **"** (*Newsweek,* 3/24/75)

◄ LITTLE KNOWN FUN FACT

◄ UNFAMILIAR QUOTATION

◄ WISHFUL THINKING DEPT.

DEPT. OF RETRACTIONS

On May 7, 1983, President Reagan conducted a telephone interview with San Antonio radio station WOAI while aboard Air Force One. During the interview, Reagan was asked about Soviet leader Yuri Andropov's proposal to count nuclear warheads instead of missile launchers. Reagan said that "if it is a real offer, I could approve it." An aide then pointed out to him that his statement contradicted the policy of his arms control experts. As the plane was landing, Reagan told the interviewer, "I may have given people the wrong impression by using the word 'approved,' and what I should have said is we're looking seriously at this to see whether it's for real or whether . . . it's just propaganda." (*Wash. Post*, 5/8/83)

Here we go again. Remember SALT II? Some people think those were real arms reduction talks, especially since that agreement called for significant reductions in arms between the superpowers. Remember Richard Nixon, Gerald Ford, Jimmy Carter? They all supported SALT II.

66 *When the United States was the only country in the world possessing these awesome weapons, we did not blackmail others with threats to use them.* 99 (3/31/83)

According to an analysis of this statement by the American Federation of Scientists, the US had an absolute nuclear weapons monopoly from 1945 until 1949, and an effective monopoly of long-range delivery systems until the early '60s. We "blackmailed others with threats" in August 1945 at Hiroshima and Nagasaki, Japan; in 1946 when Harry Truman suggested the USSR remove troops from Northern Iran; in November 1950, the day after marines were surrounded by Chinese troops at Chosen reservoir in Korea; in 1953 in an attempt by Eisenhower to get the Chinese into a settlement on Korea; in 1954 when John Foster Dulles asked the French if they'd like some awesome weapons to relieve the siege at Dien Bien Phu; in 1962, during the Cuban missile crisis.

66 *I have had some information in advance about it [the Catholic bishops' pastoral letter calling for a halt in the nuclear arms race] which indicates that it really is a legitimate effort to do exactly what we're doing. . . .* 99 (5/4/83)

Archbishop John R. Roach, president of the National Conference of Catholic Bishops, and Joseph Cardinal Bernardin, chairman of the committee drafting the bishops' letter, said they "could not accept any suggestion that there are relatively few and insignificant differences between US policies and the policies advocated in the pastoral."

GOOD-BYE, MR. KEYNES
Reagan & Economic Policy

Ronald Reagan's working model of the economy has one moving part—the free market mechanism. Strip away the heavy weight of taxes and government interference and you'll get a machine that works like crazy, churning out cars that people will always buy, steel mills that roar at full capacity, and trickle-down jobs for welfare mothers and black teenagers. But maybe the President should stop looking to the Gilded Age for inspiration. When Congress passed his tax and budget cuts nearly intact in the summer of 1981, he proclaimed that everything was in place for an economic renewal. The next month began not renewal but recession, the worst since the Great Depression. That takes some explaining. Instead we've been served up an unusually heavy dose of garbled statistics.

❝ . . . *our state has been looted and drained of its financial resources in a manner unique in our history. . . . For the last year the state has been spending $1 million a day more than it has been taking in. . . . That means that by the beginning of the next fiscal year, we will have depleted our treasury by $365 million.* **❞** (TV address, 1/30/67)

That June 30, the end of the fiscal year, a surplus appeared, right where Reagan said a deficit should be. In actual cash, it amounted to $9 million.

❝ *In 1969, 100 new 'high risk' small business firms in such fields as electronics, energy research and development, and environmental management were incorporated. But that was 10 years ago. By 1976 there was not a single new small business formation in these fields.* **❞** (Radio, Apr. 1979)

What Reagan is actually referring to is the clobbering the

DEPT. OF RETRACTIONS

In October 1982, Mr. Reagan told a state Republican party rally in Casper, Wyoming, that, "The truth is, thanks to your courage, your patience, and your support, we've already accomplished a minor miracle: we've pulled America back from the brink of [economic] disaster." Less than a month later the President seemed less sanguine. During a sound test for a radio speech, he said, "My fellow Americans, I've talked to you on a number of occasions about the economic problems and opportunities our nation faces. And I'm prepared to tell you, it's a hell of a mess." Reagan went on to ask, "We're not connected to the press now yet, are we?" He was. (*New York Times*, 11/21/82)

equity market received in the mid-'70s. It is true that new stock issues for venture capital in high technologies were zero in 1976, but that meant there were no public offerings of stock, not that there were no new businesses.

❝ *I don't think the present [auto industry] crisis is due to the importation of foreign cars. I think it is due right now to the slump in the market because of 20% interest rates [since] most people buy automobiles on the installment plan.* ❞ (Baltimore *Sun*, 4/30/80)

Reagan fails to explain in this analysis why purchasers of foreign cars don't face the same interest rates on car loans.

❝ *. . . And they say the cost of food is responsible for X percent of the increase in inflation. That cannot be laid to the farmer. The farmer has actually been over the last 20 years reducing the percentage of family income that it takes to put food on the table.* ❞ (*New York Times*, 5/1/80)

It is true that during the 1950s and '60s the percentage of the average family's income going for food dropped considerably, but that was not due to anything done by farmers. Food prices rose during that time, but incomes rose considerably more, thereby decreasing the percentage spent on food. Since 1970, that percentage has held steady at 18–20%.

❝ *Their lives [the lives of workers and their families] have been shattered by a new depression—the Carter depression. The Carter depression was created and molded by Carter himself.* ❞ (*New York Times*, 8/28/80)

Whatever Carter did mold it was not a depression, or at least not according to Reagan's own economic advisers. Alan Greenspan said, "I wouldn't have used that term." Martin

Anderson pointed out that most economists believed the nation to be in "a very severe recession." Anderson and his aides then went so far as to issue a clarification stating that "the Republican presidential nominee was not using the word 'depression' the way economists do." Oh.

66 *One day, I publicly declared that this is a depression and the President before the day was out went to the press to say, 'That shows how little he knows. This is a recession.'* **99** (*New York Times*, 10/19/80)

Not according to White House records or Reagan's staff. Said Reagan aide Lyn Nofziger: "I think it was Mondale who said that, and he didn't say it the same day. I think it was the day after, but it's good enough for us."

66 *If America can increase its savings rate by just 2 percentage points, we can add nearly $60 billion a year to our capital pool to fight high interest rates, finance new investments, new mortgages, and new jobs. I believe a country that licked the Great Depression and turned the tide in World War II can increase its savings rate by 2 percentage points—and will.* **99** (1/14/82)

◄ **WISHFUL THINKING DEPT.**

It may have been easier to win World War II. America has *never* increased its savings rate by 2 percentage points from one year to the next.

66 *In the last 10 years, federal spending has increased more than 300%.* **99** (3/15/82)

◄ **DIPSY DOODLE**

According to the 1983 budget of the United States government, federal spending (outlays) in current dollars increased by slightly more than 200% over the last 10 years. Adjusted for inflation—something Reagan always does when discussing

WISHFUL THINKING DEPT.

In a September 1982 speech before the Republican party faithful in Richmond, Virginia, the President explained, "Yes, America went backwards during those four Democratic years (1976–1980). The actual standard of living went down." Wrong again. According to Department of Commerce figures, per capita disposable income, the most precise economic measure of the standard of living, rose at an average annual rate of 1.8% during the Carter years, or nearly twice as fast as it has under Reagan in 1981–82.

the increase in military spending—federal spending has increased by 46.5%, not 300%.

66 *Real earnings are at last increasing for the first time in quite a while.* 99 (5/16/82)

Try decreasing. The Labor Department reported that in June 1982 real average weekly earnings for American workers declined 1.2%.

66 *. . . I could point to comparisons that I've been drawing up of other democracies, allies, friends of ours like our own, who are continuing down the road of intervention in business—an adversary relation with their own business community—and the comparison I'm drawing is two sets of figures. Their unemployment is greater than ours, their inflation is greater than ours.* 99 (9/28/82)

If only Reagan would go ahead with those comparisons, he'd get something more like the truth: that there's no clear link between government intervention and economic performance. Between 1970 and 1980, France's economy outperformed ours by around 41%—with a public sector some 27% larger. Germany, with one of the best inflation and employment rates for the '70s, had a public sector a third larger than America's. And Japan, with a smaller public sector than ours, somehow managed to have higher consumer inflation.

66 *For four quarters we have seen a growth in the GNP.* 99 (9/28/82)

Inflation-adjusted GNP had been declining for two of the four quarters under discussion.

The Broken Record

Ronald Reagan based his viability as a candidate for chief executive on his perfor-mance as a two-term governor of California. The state of California, enjoying an economic boom, did not noticeably suffer during his eight years at the helm. But—and this is a big but—most of Reagan's oft-repeated campaign claims of tax-cutting, welfare reform, budget trimming, etc., are not substantiated by the facts. He bandied about a lot of numbers on the campaign trails of 1976 and 1980, numbers repeat-edly disputed by California legislators, analysts, and journalists. But correction has never been enough to unstick the needle in the groove of Reagan misstatement. As president, he continues to cite as justification for current administration policy those same old non-accomplishments from the California record.

❝ *In California, with some realistic rules about determining eligibility, we reduced the [welfare] roles by more than 300,000 people in three years.* **❞** *(U.S. News & World Report, 5/31/76)*

The Welfare Reform Act of 1971 was Reagan's most heralded success. Campaign literature said it "best exemplifies his qualities as governor and as a leader." The precise number of reduced recipients claimed varies from 340,000 to 360,000. The Reform Act was responsible for only a small part of that reduction. The Institute of Business and Economic Research of the University of California at Berkeley concludes that the Act actually helped strike about 17,000 from the rolls. Outside factors must be given credit for the balance: the Therapeutic Abortion Act, which Reagan signed; a national trend toward smaller welfare families; a steadily improving (post-1970–71 recession) economy; and liberalized federal law. In fact, if you want to play a numbers game, just subtract the caseload low of 2,060,875 (from the January after Reagan left office) from

SPECIAL REPORT #3

the caseload high of 2,292,945 (from six months before the reform became law) and you get a grand total caseload reduction of 232,070—only 2,070 more than the total number of Medicaid abortions in the same time period. Or, as state legislative analyst A. Alan Post put it, "The chiselers he is talking about are unborn children."

❝ *We reformed welfare in California and we saved $2 billion for the taxpayers over a three-year period. . . .* ❞ (*Wash. Star,* 3/2/80)

There was never $2 billion to save. That figure represents money that would have been spent had the number of people receiving welfare continued to increase, even after the recession ended and the rate of abortion increased. Anthony Beilenson (D-Cal.) used these same calculations to figure out that by 1978 55% of the state's population would be on the dole; and that by 1984 everyone in the state of California, including the governor, would be on welfare. This claim sometimes appeared as "We *returned* $2 billion to the taxpayer," which is even more wrong.

❝ *We funneled 76,000 welfare recipients through that program [CWEP] into private enterprise and took them permanently off the welfare rolls. They're out there taking care of themselves now.* ❞ (*Wash. Star,* 3/2/80)

The California Work Experience Program (CWEP) "put to work" only 4,760 welfare recipients—the figure of 76,000 refers to the number of people who left welfare to go to work regardless of whether the state helped them or not. A state legislative staff survey found that only 262 CWEP workers went into "private enterprise"—mostly as farm workers. This

55

unimpressive performance led the state legislature to vote to abolish the program, a move Reagan vetoed in 1974.

❝ . . . *because I don't think government has a right to take one dollar more than government needs, we gave the surpluses back to the people in the form of tax rebates. We gave back over eight years $5.7 billion to the people of California. We stopped the bureaucracy dead in its tracks, the same way I would like to stop it at its national level.* **❞** (*Wash. Post*, 4/27/80)

Reagan campaigned as "the greatest tax-cutter in the state's history" when, in fact, he was the greatest tax-hiker. The portion of the budget over which the governor has the most control—operations—increased under Reagan from $2.2 billion to $3.5 billion. State income tax revenues quadrupled, sales tax income tripled, and property tax revenue more than doubled. Reagan enacted the largest single tax hike in California history—a $1 billion omnibus tax rate increase. Tax brackets were narrowed in order to soak middle-class taxpayers. The top personal income tax went from 7% to 11%. The "rebates" consisted of shifting the incidence of taxation and redistributing revenues to local government—very little actually went back to taxpayers. As for the stopped-dead bureaucracy: the state budget more than doubled, going from $4.6 billion to $10.2 billion. One analyst put the eight-year increase in real terms as 85%. The number of state employees rose by 5.7% (in the same period, the number of federal civilian employees declined by more than 3%). In fact, the state coffers swelled with a surplus from all this increased taxation, a surplus that eventually spurred the populace into the tax-revolt known as Proposition 13.

❝ *Mr. Ford is overlooking a certain factor and that is that in 1966, I won the governorship in a state that is almost two-to-*

In October 1973, Governor Reagan was vigorously promoting a referendum that would implement his planned reform of property and income taxes. He personally canvassed the state of California to drum up support. In the final days of this effort, a television reporter asked him, "Do you think the average voter really understands the language of this proposition?" Reagan replied, "No, he shouldn't try, I don't either." Proposition 1 lost three days later.

one Democratic by a million votes and was re-elected by almost as many. 99 (*New York Times,* 3/3/80)

That "almost as many" was 497,000—otherwise known as half as many.

66 *And without exception in eight years, I took my appointments [to judgeships] from those who were rated [by review committees] as 'exceptionally well qualified.'* 99 (*New York Times,* 10/15/80)

Not quite. When the committees opposed his selection of aide William P. Clark, Jr., to California's highest court, Reagan made the appointment anyway. Clark eventually became President Reagan's National Security adviser, and later his Interior Secretary.

TROJAN HORSES
Reagan & Taxes

Ronald Reagan pins the whole mess on Karl Marx. First, the bearded economist gave us Soviet Russia. Then, to put an extra nail in the coffin, he sent us the graduated income tax, and taxes are the number-one swindle in the eyes of the President. Why, he asks, do politicians think they can spend *our* money better than *we* can? Maybe the President has mixed up his centuries. In the old days monarchs did exact tribute, so they could build pyramids and castles, but nowadays the federal government spends *our* money on roads and schools. Conversely, a basic premise of Reaganomics is that sharply reduced taxes would make our economy walk again. But corporate taxes fell from 30% to 12% of all federal government revenues between 1950 and 1980, and we've been through several recessions in that time. Of course, this is merely fact. And since when did the President ever let facts get in the way of a good argument?

> **"** *This whole progressive tax system is a* foreign import— *spawned by Karl Marx a century ago. He viewed it as one of the prime essentials of a socialist state. He said that in imposing socialism on a people, the progressive income tax should be used to 'tax the middle class out of existence.'* **"** (*Screen Actor,* Sept. 1959)

> **TALL TALE**

Karl Marx is not the architect of our tax system, although in two lines in *The Communist Manifesto* he did say a graduated income tax would be an instrument of socialist policy.

The progressive income tax evolved gradually in the US from the income tax created during the Civil War. The 16th Amendment legalized the income tax, and the Act of 1913 provided its first progressive features. This legislation drew its inspiration from two economic philosophers, William Stanley Jevons (an Englishman) and Karl Menger (an Austrian).

Q: "Knowing of your great distaste for taxes and tax increases, can you assure the American people now that you'll flatly rule out any tax increase, revenue enhancers, or, specifically, an increase in the gas tax?"
A: "Unless there's a palace coup and I'm over-taken—or overthrown, no, I don't see the necessity for that." (9/28/82)

Q: "Mr. President, at your last news conference, you said it would take a palace coup for you to approve a $.05 a gallon increase in gasoline. . . . Have you changed your mind?"
A: "I don't think that I said it with reference to that. I said that on a general subject of tax increases, as such, it would take a palace coup." (11/11/82)

The President proposed the gas tax legislation to Congress on 11/30/82; he signed it into law on 1/6/83.

To them, the progressive income tax was the guarantee of a bourgeois society—it spread the tax burden equitably without destroying free market activity. The idea of the progressive tax as a bludgeon for the middle class was quite far from their minds.

❝ *What Congress, when they finished, gave him [Kennedy] was 30% [in tax cuts] at the bottom levels of the income earners and 23% at the top levels, and it averaged out to 27%. So . . . Kemp-Roth is asking for exactly what, in amount, Kennedy asked for.* ❞ (CBS Network News, 4/3/80)

Not exactly. In 1963, JFK requested a tax cut of 18%, weighted in favor of lower- and middle-income families. After his death, Congress enacted a 19% tax cut.

❝ *History shows that when the taxes of a nation approach about 20% of the people's income, there begins to be a lack of respect for government. . . . When it reaches 25% there comes an increase in lawlessness.* ❞ (Time, 4/14/80)

History shows no such thing. Income tax rates in Europe have traditionally been far higher than US rates, while European crime rates have been much lower.

❝ *The percentage of your earnings the federal government took in taxes in 1960 has almost doubled.* ❞ (2/5/81)

No. As a share of personal income, federal individual income taxes were 10.4% in 1960 and 12.0% in 1981.

❝ *The bipartisan [tax cut] proposal was designed to encourage small businesses. . . .* ❞ (7/27/81)

If so, the proposal was poorly designed. About 80% of the

Accelerated Cost Recovery System cut in corporate taxes were to go to the top one tenth of 1% of America's businesses, or those "small businesses" with assets of more than $250 million. Said William Hardman, a representative of the Small Business Legislative Council, "It would be difficult to write a tax bill better designed to speed the extinction of small business."

❝ *I mentioned the tax cuts in Coolidge's era. Every one of those tax cuts resulted in more revenues for the government because of the increased prosperity of the country as a whole.* **❞** (5/28/81)

◄ TALL TALE

How about mentioning that in 1923, 1924, and 1927—when Coolidge was president—cuts in federal income tax rates led to a decrease in federal revenues. By 1929, the end of President Coolidge's terms in office, total Internal Revenue collections had dropped to $2.9 billion, down from $3.2 billion in 1922, the year before Coolidge took office.

❝ *Now, some of our business tax cuts are retroactive and go back to January 1, but, of course, they won't be felt until tax-paying time.* **❞** (*Wash. Post,* 10/1/81)

But, of course, some impact should already have been felt. Tax-paying time for businesses, as we hope the President is aware, comes every three months. According to the staff of the Congressional Joint Committee on Taxation, business tax breaks had already cost the government $1.6 billion in fiscal 1981.

❝ *As a matter of fact, if anyone wants to look closely, our original tax plan did not contain the reduction of the 70% bracket. That was suggested by the Democrats.* **❞** (11/12/81)

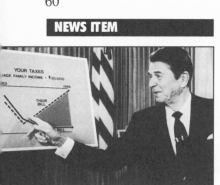

During the 1981 tax fight, Reagan displayed on television a numberless chart indicating a huge gap between the Reagan tax cut and the tax cut proposed by the Democrats. Actually, by 1986, a one-earner family would be paying $2,168 in taxes under his plan and $2,385 under the Democrats', a difference of only $217. Explaining the chart, Karna Small, deputy White House press secretary, said, "The President wanted to keep it as simple as possible."

No it wasn't. The original Reagan tax plan called for a lowering of the top rates from 70% to 50%, to be phased in over a period of three years. As David Stockman so memorably explained, "Kemp-Roth [the original GOP tax reduction proposal] was always a Trojan horse to bring down the top rate."

❝ *But I also happen to be someone who believes in tithing—the giving of a tenth [to charity].* ❞ (1/19/82)

He may believe, but he doesn't give. Larry Speakes informed the press the following day that the Reagans' total current charitable giving—$5,965 in cash contributions—did not approach 10% of total income. It was, in fact, more like 1.4%.

❝ *I would like to have them [the critics of his tax plan] give a specific on where this is a budget for the rich. The bulk of the personal income tax cut goes right across from the lower income to middle America.* ❞ (2/8/82)

Well, here are some specifics. According to the Congressional Budget Office, 35.1% of the tax cuts go to the wealthiest 5% of the taxpayers. The *National Journal,* using CBO and Census Bureau information, estimated that, had the 1983 tax cuts gone into effect in 1981, they would have taken $1.2 billion from the poorest fifth of the income spectrum and added $36 billion to the incomes of the richest fifth.

❝ *I would like to quote a few words by a very famous and celebrated orator, journalist, soldier, historian, and statesman. People have even said he might have made a great actor if he tried that. Winston Churchill. He said, 'The idea that a nation can tax itself into prosperity is one of the crudest delusions which has ever befuddled the human mind.' Now I don't know how that quote happened to catch my eye.* ❞ (3/9/82)

Neither does anyone else. Reagan's speechwriters "don't know where he got that one from." Nor does the British historian at the Library of Congress; there was no such passage in the Library's extensive collection of Churchill quotations. Ten other books of quotations also failed to provide a clue.

A tax shelter is only a shelter if you lose your investment. . . . And the fact is that, like so many others who have gone into government service, [William French Smith's tax shelter] was done by someone the Attorney General trusts to handle the investments he might have. (5/24/82)

A tax shelter permits you to take special tax writeoffs whether or not your investment earns a return. Reagan was also incorrect in blaming an investment counselor for the financial maneuver that converted a $16,500 investment into $66,000 in tax deductions—Smith's own office admitted two weeks before the President spoke that Smith "did it himself despite his blind trust that holds his assets."

Justice Oliver Wendell Holmes once said, 'Keep the government poor and remain free.' (6/15/82)

An official at the White House speechwriting office says the President "came up with that one himself. Holmes never said anything point-blank exactly like that . . . we're still trying to track it down." Professor Ed Bander of Suffolk Law School in Boston, a recognized Holmes scholar, didn't think Holmes "ever said anything that I can see which resembles that quote."

DEPT. OF RETRACTIONS

Speaking to the Massachusetts High Technology Council in Bedford, Massachusetts, the President surprised everybody when he asked, "But when are we all going to have the courage to point out that, in our tax structure, the corporate tax is very hard to justify. . . ." (1/26/83) Later that afternoon, a White House spokesman assured members of the press that "we're not seriously considering" repealing the corporate tax.

◀ UNFAMILIAR QUOTATION

Know Thine Own Ad Campaign

The following exchange, on the subject of the Reagan tax cut, took place on ABC's "Issues and Answers" between interviewers John Laurence and Bob Clark and candidate Reagan. The line of questioning quickly veered from the candidate's tax policy to the candidate's ability to remember his own television commercials. Lost in the shuffle was the fact that, even if he could remember what he was saying, it was incorrect—there never was a Kennedy "30% federal tax cut that became law." (Source: *The New Yorker*, 3/31/80)

JL: "You've been saying that you didn't always agree with President Kennedy, but that he found that a 30% tax cut helped almost everybody in the country, and if you were elected President you would cut taxes the same way he did."

RR: *"No, I didn't know what the rate of his tax cut was. I said that he went for a broad-based cut in the income tax. I don't know what the percent of that cut was but that it was contrary to all the economic advice being given and that it did result in an increase in revenues."*

JL: "If I can quote from your own ad, you're saying on camera 'I didn't always agree with President Kennedy, but when his 30% federal tax cut became law, the economy did so well that every group in the country came out ahead. If I become President, we're going to try that again.' Do you remember saying those words?"

RR: *"I don't remember saying that, because I honestly don't* know what the rate of the tax cut was."

JL: "Well, perhaps someone else wrote them for you?"

RR: *"I'm sure they did. But I don't even remember reading that."*

BC: "Coincidentally, I saw them in print this week, with your media adviser—fellow who puts together your media commercials—giving out the text, I believe."

JL: "Well, that raises the whole question of how familiar you are with the television ads that you do and . . ."

RR: *"Sure, I do them. I read them. And I suppose in the process of a whole afternoon, as you know, sitting in front of the camera and doing these things, and each one several times over, that I maybe just went by that one without thinking the 30% figure was familiar to me."*

Q: "Governor, did you pay any state income tax by the April 15 deadline?"

A (Obviously surprised): "You know something. I don't actually know whether I did or not." (Press conference, 5/4/71)

He hadn't.

The Balancing Act

❝ *But I don't find any room for me in a debate on whether the deficit should be $52 billion or $70 or $80 billion. . . . That size deficit is extremely dangerous and will put us back on the inflationary spiral.* ❞ (*Newsweek*, 3/24/75)

❝ *We have no choice. This government must get back as quickly as possible to a balanced budget.* ❞ (*New York Times*, 11/21/75)

❝ *. . . I don't know whether it [a balanced budget] is political or not, but it is absolutely necessary.* ❞ (*Wash. Post*, 1/12/76)

❝ *Balancing the budget by cutting the cost of government is the Republican way.* ❞ (*Wash. Star*, 6/13/78)

❝ *With only a 2% reduction in spending, we would have a balanced federal budget.* ❞ (*Savannah* [Ga.] *News*, 3/2/80)

❝ *I believe the budget can be balanced by 1982 or 1983.* ❞ (9/21/80)

❝ *I have submitted an economic plan that I have worked out in concert with a number of fine economists in this country, all of whom approve it and believe . . . that it can provide for a balanced budget by 1983 if not earlier. . . .* ❞ (Presidential debate, 10/28/80)

❝ *I'm as committed today as on the first day I took office to balancing the budget.* ❞ (9/15/81)

❝ *This administration is committed to a balanced budget, and we will fight to the last blow to achieve it by 1984.* ❞ (9/21/81)

❝ *In the first place, I said that [a balanced budget] was our goal, not a promise.* ❞ (12/17/81)

THE BOTTOMLESS LINE
Reagan & the Deficit

I t just keeps getting bigger. Reagan campaigned as a budget trimmer, but a look at his record as governor of California (see Special Report #3) shows that he hasn't always kept that promise in the past. John Anderson kept asking Reagan how he was going to cut taxes, increase defense spending, and balance the budget all at the same time. Now we know the answer. On taking office, Reagan declared with his customary certainty that "the only cause of inflation is all those federal deficits." Now we have lower inflation *and* higher deficits. Hmmm. The situation definitely calls for Ronald Reagan's special math. It's time to get on national television and shuffle some charts and diagrams around, throw out a bunch of numbers and percentages and comparisons—and hope that nobody in the home audience has the time to calculate whether any of the facts and figures are true. Meanwhile, the literal-minded among us are faced with an odd situation: The same president who supports a balanced budget amendment to the US Constitution heads the administration with the biggest federal budget deficits in American history. Hmmm.

" *Mr. Carter is acting as if he hasn't been in charge for the past three and a half years; as if someone else was responsible for the largest deficit in American history.* **"** (Nationally televised campaign speech, 10/24/80)

Federal deficits totaled $195 billion under Mr. Carter. The latest budget projections suggest that during Mr. Reagan's six years the deficit will total nearly $1 *trillion.*

" *Yes, there'll be a $45 billion deficit, but just think what that means. That means that that deficit would be double that without our program.* **"** (3/3/81)

The 1982 budget deficit was more than double $45 billion *with* the President's program. At $110.6 billion, it was the largest deficit in history. Budget projections based on the Congressional Budget Office's data suggest that the cumulative deficit accrued during Reagan's four years will nearly equal the cumulative deficits accrued since the beginning of the Republic in 1789.

DIPSY DOODLE

❝And already, we can tell you that that $90 billion deficit of 1983 will actually be smaller in proportion to the GNP than the deficits were in 1975–1978. . . . ❞ (3/8/82)

Sounds good, doesn't it? Unfortunately, the figures tell a different story. The 1983 deficit was in fact 6.1% of GNP, which makes it larger, not smaller, than percentages of GNP for any single year between 1975 and 1978: 3.1% in 1975; 4.0% in 1976; 2.4% in 1977; 2.3% in 1978. In fact, when the House Budget Committee ranked post–World War II deficits as a percentage of GNP, Reagan's budgets for his term in office took four of the top five spots.

❝Our original [budget cuts] totaled $101 billion. . . . Our own representation from the Congress proposed compromising at $60 billion. Their counterparts from the Democratic side of the aisle proposed $35 billion. ❞ (4/29/82)

House Budget Committee aides say that Reagan's $35 billion Democratic figure arbitrarily included only two categories of domestic spending: non-COLA (Cost of Living Adjusted) entitlements and non-defense discretionary appropriations. When other deficit-reducing methods are included—defense cuts, tax revenues, user fees—the Democrats' proposed deficit reduction is far greater than that proposed by the President or the Republicans. The Democrats' proposal would cut the deficit on average $135 billion a year for three years, while the Republicans would cut it by $121 billion, and Reagan by only $79 billion.

66 *We managed in less than one year to substantially slow the momentum of decades of growth in government. The new management of a failing company that made changes like this in only one year would soon be the talk of Wall Street.* **99** (5/4/82)

Any company that increased its deficit by some $200 billion in two years would soon be bankrupt.

66 *The budget deficits, I don't think can be laid at any individual's door. We have—I could turn around and say how much less that deficit would be if the Democratic leadership that is now pointing this nice little thrust . . . if they had given us all that we asked for last year. . . .* **99** *(Wash. Post, 7/29/82)*

◄ WISHFUL THINKING DEPT.

Earlier, before the deficits skyrocketed, Reagan thought they had given him all he asked for: "On behalf of the administration, let me say we embrace and fully support that bi-partisan substitute [Gramm-Latta Amendment]. It will achieve all the essential aims of controlling government spending, reducing the tax burden, building a national defense second to none, and stimulating growth and creating millions of new jobs." (4/28/81) And after the 1981 tax cut was passed, Reagan was asked, "Sir, have you now got your program in place? Ought it now to work the way you envision it?" Answered the President, "Yes." (7/29/81)

66 *A propaganda campaign would have you believe these deficits are caused by our so-called massive tax cut and defense buildup. Well, that's a real dipsy doodle, because even after our tax cuts are fully in place, they will barely neutralize the enormous Social Security tax increase approved in 1977. . . . Current and projected deficits result from sharp increases in non-defense spending.* **99** (11/16/82)

◄ DIPSY DOODLE

There he goes again. The 1981 tax cut will cut revenues by *$377 billion* over the 1982–85 period, while increased revenues from Social Security and Medicare taxes will be only *$78 billion*—the government loses *$299 billion*. Ignoring the effects of inflation, the only areas of growth aside from defense are interest on the debt, Social Security, Medicare, and other health and pension programs. In fact, according to a *Washington Post* analysis, if defense spending and taxes are kept at the levels proposed by the President, all federal programs except Social Security and other pensions, the court system, and a few other basic functions will have to be *terminated* in order to balance the budget by 1985.

WANT ADS
Reagan & Unemployment

Jobs, jobs, jobs. In 1980, Reagan was handing out promises to the unemployed like campaign bumper stickers. He just couldn't say often enough how badly he felt for the "common man" whose job was a casualty of the "Carter depression." Then he got elected. And one of the opening salvos of his administration was a bid to shorten the time covered by unemployment insurance—just as unemployment was increasing in volume and duration. As it reached double digits, Reagan unfurled want ads from the Sunday paper. The problem, he sought to explain, was not jobs, jobs, jobs, but able-bodied men (and he meant just men) willing to fill them. The plain truth is that since Reagan got _his_ job, three million Americans have lost theirs.

◄ TALL TALE

66 *We have reduced the number of employees by 2½% without a layoff or firing.* 99 (Speech, Kansas State University, 10/26/67)

The California Mental Hygiene Department had laid off at least 200 people by July 1 of that year. The Department of Health had fired 250. That's 450 former state employees who would dispute the "without a layoff or firing" claim.

66 *He [a Detroit steelworker] invited me to come to his back-yard for hot dogs, and he invited in some of his friends and neighbors, all of them unemployed automobile industry, steel, and construction workers.* 99 (*New York Times*, 10/19/80)

The steelworker was invited to invite the candidate into his backyard by the candidate's public relations staff. Half of those present had jobs. During the campaign Reagan was often tempted to exaggerate the level of unemployment—about 7.5%

66 *Unemployment insurance is a pre-paid vacation for freeloaders.* 99 (Sacramento *Bee*, 4/28/66)

❝As far as I am concerned, the line between depression and recession cannot be measured in strict economists' terms but must be measured in human terms. When our working people— including those who are unemployed—must endure the worst misery since the 1930s, then I think we ought to recognize that they consider it a depression.❞ (Wash. Post, 8/26/80)

WISHFUL THINKING DEPT.

at the time of this statement. Since his election he seems better able to resist that particular temptation.

❝If you'll remember, there were two million who lost their jobs in the last six months of 1980, during the election. . . .❞ (1/8/82)

The number of people employed *increased* in the last six months of 1980, ending the year with 283,000 more people working than in July.

❝I realize there's been an increase in unemployment. It's been a continuation of an increase that got underway in the last several months of 1980.❞ (1/19/82)

Still wrong. In the last six months of 1980, unemployment declined from 7.8% to 7.3%. It declined further to 7.2% in July 1981, before beginning the climb to double-digit figures.

❝There's a million more people working than there were in 1980.❞ (1/19/82)

For the President to use absolute figures is misleading—the work force is always expanding, and so it is the *percentage* of unemployed people that is the critical figure. Anyway, he still got it wrong—according to the Bureau of Labor Statistics, there were only 27,000 more people employed in December 1981 than there were in December 1980.

❝Well, one of the things that's needed was illustrated in the local paper on Sunday. I made it a point to count the number of pages of help-wanted ads in this time of great unemployment. There were 24 full pages of classified ads of employers looking for employees.❞ (1/19/82)

This is not the first time that Reagan has pulled this "want ads" trick. After he alluded to 33½ pages of want ads in the Sunday *Washington Post* of March 15, 1981, the American Vocation Association analyzed the section. That organization found that nearly all of the 2,000 jobs listed required some kind of vocational training and approximately 85% required a high level of training. The association concluded that high unemployment rates and lots of want ads in Sunday papers only served to highlight the mismatch between current worker skills and marketplace needs.

66 *We have, in some of the hardest-hit states, extended the unemployment insurance. There's nothing that strikes to my heart more than the unemployed. . . .* **99** (3/31/82)

Then how come the Labor Department estimates that changes in the eligibility formula in the 1981 budget reduced extended benefits for 1.5 million jobless workers? Moreover, changes in the way a state becomes eligible for the extended benefit program had Michigan—the hardest hit of the states—thrown off that program for 13 weeks just prior to the President's heartfelt speech.

66 *When . . . individuals charge [that] our administration fights inflation by putting people out of work, I say they're exploiting helpless people for political gain. It's the most cynical form of demagoguery.* **99** (9/25/82)

Some of those "demagogues" are the President's top advisers: Treasury Secretary Donald Regan ("All I know is that our economy is slowing down and I think that's healthy, because we have to slow the economy down in order to get some of the inflation out of it"); Commerce Secretary Malcolm Baldridge ("A slight recession, I think, is almost necessary right now"); Council of Economic Advisers Chairman-designate

NEWS ITEM

In mid-April 1982, the President told a class of Illinois schoolchildren that unemployment had declined by 88,000 in March 1982. This contradicted the Bureau of Labor Statistics, whose figures showed that seasonally adjusted unemployment had *increased* in March by 279,000, to 9% of the work force. The White House explained that Reagan was referring to "raw" figures, before seasonal adjustments had been factored in by the Bureau.

DIPSY DOODLE

66 *Is it news that some fellow out in South Succotash someplace has just been laid off?* **99** (3/16/82)

❝If all of the unemployed today were in a single line allowing two feet for each of them, that line would reach from New York City to Los Angeles, California. All of this can be cured and all of it can be solved.❞ (Presidential debate, 10/28/80)

Martin Feldstein ("Extremists among both the supply-siders and monetarists who predicted that inflation would be reduced without raising unemployment have been decisively proven wrong"); presidential spokesman Larry Speakes ("[High unemployment] is the price you have to pay for bringing inflation down"); Office of Management and Budget Director David Stockman (high unemployment is "part of the cure, not the problem").

❝I would also like to point out that there's a higher percentage of . . . employed today than has been true even in the past in times of full employment.❞ (9/28/82)

How about pointing out that the Bureau of Labor Statistics employment/population ratio, which measures the percentage of population over 16 years of age that is employed, was at 57% in September 1982 as against a high of 59.2% in 1979?

❝We have been . . . increasing unemployment steadily . . . for probably a decade and a half. But it became very pronounced in the years between—well, from '77 through 1980 and then on into the depths of this recession.❞ (10/4/82)

Unemployment in 1975 was 8.5%; in 1980, it was 7.1%. It became "very pronounced" in 1982, when it averaged 9.7%.

❝No, I want to be fair. Unemployment is 9.8%. When we took office it was 7.4%. Okay, I'll take blame for 2.4% of the unemployment. And if, as everybody is worried about, it goes to 10%, well then I'll take blame for 2.6%.❞ (10/6/82)

Let's be fair to everyone. In the past 30 years, here's how the unemployment rate changed during each president's term in office. Republicans: Ike, +3.7%; Nixon, +2.0%; Ford, +3.1%; Reagan, +2.4%. Democrats: JFK, −.9%; LBJ,

−2.3%; Carter, −.1%. It's hard to see why the Democrats should accept blame for 7.4% unemployment, when Republican presidents have always increased unemployment and Democratic presidents have always decreased it. Unemployment passed the 10% mark two days after the President's speech.

WISHFUL THINKING DEPT.

❝ *But if a lot of businesses would take a look and see if they could hire just one person, it would be interesting to see how much we can reduce these unemployment rolls. . . . If everyone would just simply look at it from the standpoint there are more businesses in the United States than there are unemployed.* ❞ (12/23/82)

Recalling Reagan's unemployment solution, a reporter covering the President's fly-in to Louisiana to inspect flood damage came up with this proposal: "If everyone on the trip would just take one bucket of water home and flush it down the toilet, we could solve the flooding problem."

TALL TALE

❝ *I have a special reason for wanting to solve this [unemployment] problem in a lasting way. I was 21 and looking for work in 1932, one of the worst years of the Great Depression.* ❞ (10/13/82)

According to *Reagan,* Lou Cannon's biography of Ronald Reagan, about two months after graduating from college the 21-year-old Reagan found work as a radio announcer, earning $100 a month. Soon after, his salary was raised to $300 a month, more than double the highest salary his father had ever earned.

AWFULLY LARGE OFFICES
Reagan & Big Government

A big fan of big government Ronald Reagan is not. "Get government off the back of business," he preaches. In this crusade, Washington, D.C., becomes a modern-day Babylon, crawling with regulatory sins and sinners. The deadliest sins: paperwork (all those government forms) and regulations (all those government rules). The most reprehensible sinners: EPA, OSHA, Highway Safety, FDA, and, in days of yore, HEW. "You don't have to spend much time in Washington to appreciate the prophetic vision of the man who designed all the streets going around in circles," Reagan quips. But then he didn't like Sacramento either. This loathing for government, this eagerness to prove that any program to aid the disadvantaged is nothing but a boondoggle and a money gobbler, leads him to contrive statistics and stories with unmatched vigor. The anti-government, anti-regulation, anti-Washington stance is the perfect vehicle for the righteous indignation Reagan is so good at. It is also the inspiration for some of his greatest gaffes.

❝ *Fascism's private ownership, private enterprise, but [with] total government control and regulation. Well, isn't this the liberal philosophy?* **❞**
(*Newsweek*, 1/12/76)

❝ *Today, no one denies the American people would resist the nationalization of industry. But in defiance of this attitude, the federal government owns and operates more than 19,000 businesses.* **❞** (*L.A. Times*, 1/3/62)

If that number ever reached a thousand, Reagan would be lucky. The federal government has formed a number of corporations and enterprises—the Tennessee Valley Authority, the Saint Lawrence Seaway Corporation, the Export-Import Bank, the Government National Mortgage Association. No one knows for sure how many there really are; in its study of government enterprises and corporations, the National Academy of Public Administration never mentions more than a few hundred.

❝ *It is estimated that small businessmen in America spend a* *total of 130 million man-hours a year filling out government required forms.* **"** (Debate, 9/11/75)

In 1977, the Small Business Administration estimated that there were 5.978 million small businesses in America—making those back-breaking paperwork requirements an average of only 21.76 hours per business per year.

" *At one stage, some years ago, GE [General Electric] could produce light bulbs for half the price at which it was selling them and was in open competition with Sylvania and Westinghouse and all the others. But GE already had such a large share of the market that it didn't dare reduce the price as low as it could have, because if it captured any more of the market, it could have been in trouble with the government.* **"** *(Wash. Post, 6/3/76)*

GE spokesman William J. Barron: ". . . we are wholly unable to identify any single system . . . which had the effect of cutting in half the cost of manufacturing our household-type lamp bulbs."

" *I bet everyone in this room has, at one time or another, climbed a ladder. How we did it without their [OSHA's] 144 rules and regulations about ladder-climbing I'll never know.* **"** *(Sanford [Me.] Journal Tribune, 2/10/78)*

OSHA has two regulations on climbing ladders.

" *The Senate Energy and Natural Resources Committee has unanimously approved legislation which first confesses that in 1893 the US minister to the Kingdom of Hawaii did "unlawfully conspire" to overthrow the government of Queen Liliuokalani. It then goes on to set up an Aboriginal Hawaiian Claims Settlement Study commission. This commission will seek out*

NEWS ITEM

According to a February 26, 1966, story in the *Los Angeles Times,* Reagan, on his mismanagement-in-government high horse, asserted that as a result of state regulations, the California Board of Education would have to burn $180,000 worth of extra state-printed textbooks. Two days later State Board of Education president Thomas Braden pointed out that the textbooks in question would, on the contrary, *never* be burned. They would either be re-adopted, distributed as extra allotments, or donated overseas.

◀ **TALL TALE**

At a news conference in late May 1983, President Reagan pointed to Morris High School in the Bronx, New York, and the Johnston High School in Austin, Texas, as examples of what can be done to improve public education without federal intervention. But Morris High School principal Frances Vazquez says she hired 16 remedial reading teachers with funds from a Great Society Program. "If we didn't have these teachers it would be devastating," she adds. Adan C. Salgado, Johnston's principal, was also a little surprised by the President's comments. "He did not really understand our situation. He did not have all the facts."

No kidding. Reagan managed to ignore both a 1980 federal desegregation order and $3.4 million in emergency federal aid to the Austin district, both

descendants of the aboriginal Hawaiians and bestow on them a billion dollars. **99** (Radio, Feb. 1978)

Apparently a reference to legislation that, in December 1980, became Public Law #96-565. It authorized the Native Hawaiians Study Commission to look into the needs of native Hawaiians and, by June 1983, write a report with recommendations to the Senate. The Commission is not authorized to bestow one red cent.

66 *This one I'm sure will touch your heart. The health planners in Washington are determined to cut public health care costs by reducing 'unnecessary surgery.' According to them, that term fits such things as cataract operations and hysterectomies. However, if a man agrees to dress in women's clothes for a year the Public Health Service says Medicare should pay for his 'gender reassignment surgery.'* **99** (Radio, June 1978)

The health planners were suggesting that *some* of these oft-performed hysterectomy and cataract operations *might be* unnecessary and were therefore recommending a "second opinion" policy. As for transsexual surgery, the Public Health Service was not able to produce any evidence of an official recommendation; the Department of Health and Welfare, which oversees Medicare and Medicaid, considers such surgery "experimental" and thus not eligible for benefit coverage. An official at the Department did point out that as Medicare is for those 65 and over, the number of interested men would be minimal.

66 *Do you remember that our government some time ago appropriated money to go into the automobile business—well at least for one car? The idea was that Washington could build a safe, non-polluting, economical, high-gas-mileage car to prove the automobile industry could (if they would) produce such cars* *using existing technology. Well, Secretary of Transportation Brock Adams has unveiled the Department's $250,000 ideal car. . . . According to the Secretary and Joan Claybrook, administrator of the National Highway Transportation Safety Agency, the government had proven that the automobile industry could achieve all of the federally mandated requirements if it really wanted to. Indeed, Ms. Claybrook made a speech to the Economics Club of Detroit claiming the $250,000 car could be produced at roughly present day production costs. But guess what? The magic car has never been tested to see if all those accolades and statistics are true. The California company that did the job for the government says there was no money in the budget for testing. The Secretary is blaming Ms. Claybrook and Ms. Claybrook's staff says she was not fully briefed and that her claims were—well— exaggerated.* **"** (Radio, June 1978)

NEWS ITEM CONT.

of which Mr. Salgado considered crucial to the improved performance of his students. The President's willful misapprehension of the federal role in public education was too much for the *New York Times,* which found Reagan to be "as oblivious to contradiction and rebuttal as a tape cassette."

Reagan is referring to a $12 million program—which included money for testing—that aimed to produce cars, called research safety vehicles, in designs that would meet current Detroit production capabilities and 1985 federal highway safety standards. Several models were produced, one of them a redesigned 1977 Chevrolet intended to demonstrate that the era of the family car need not crumble in the face of safety and emission goals. The model was designed to meet certain specifications—just as cars in Detroit are—and was tested as it was being assembled—just as cars in Detroit are. At least 17 vehicles were assembled, not just one. In early summer 1978, members of Congress asked to see one of the cars, although final testing had not yet been done. This is where Reagan got the never-been-tested allegation. However, the car was subsequently tested and, as advertised, got 27½ miles per gallon, and crashed safely at 40 miles per hour. Another model, composed of several different Detroit-made cars, got 33 mpg, crashed safely at 50 mph, and met 1985

Reagan said in Michigan that too much regulation was the "major reason" that Chrysler needed federal aid to avert bankruptcy. When asked to name some of these regulations, he responded: "Well, there are tens and tens of thousands of unnecessary regulations. I think that someone could list off some to begin with that have been mandated, but I don't think that would be the answer." (*New York Times*, 5/16/80)

DIPSY DOODLE ➤

emission standards. The National Highway Traffic Safety Administration believed it had the potential for saving half of the gas used in 1978 and some 15,000 lives. Cars of that design were given to the French, German, and Japanese equivalents of Detroit, all of whom tested and found that it lived up to or exceeded claims. Needless to say, Mrs. Claybrook's staff never said either that she was not fully briefed or that the claims for the car were exaggerated.

❝ *It is reported that General Motors now has more than 20,000 full-time employees who don't help build automobiles. They just work on federal paperwork and regulations.* **❞** (Radio, Jan. 1979)

According to GM, about 5,000 employees—out of more than 500,000—are involved to some degree in government "paperwork," mostly on things like taxes. Reagan used this statistic constantly on the campaign trail in 1980. When told by interviewer Bill Plante that GM said it had 24,000 employees working on government-mandated programs, most of them as designers and engineers, and only 5,000 on forms, Reagan responded, "I should not have been saying it as I did and it disturbed me somewhat. I haven't heard any criticism of that one, but I thought, just doing paperwork it sounded like an awfully large office."

❝ *There has actually been an increase in the number of accidents under OSHA.* **❞** (*Wash. Post*, 1/25/80)

There's also been an increase in the total number of people at work—again, it's not absolute numbers but percentages that matter. And the number of deaths, injuries, and illnesses per 100 full-time workers declined from 10.9 in 1972, the first full year of OSHA's operation, to 8.7 in 1980.

❝ *When Chicago burned down they didn't declare it a disaster area. They just rebuilt it, the people of Chicago, and this is the kind of America we can have again.* **❞** (*Wash. Star,* 3/2/80)

This is the kind of America we've had all along: On October 10, 1871, the Secretary of War, General William W. Balknap, declared the Chicago fire "a national calamity." The mayor of Chicago gave absolute police authority to the US Army under Lieutenant General Philip H. Sheridan. Federal rations, tents, and other supplies arrived from all over the country. According to A. T. Andreas, author of *History of Chicago,* millions of dollars to aid the rebuilding of Chicago came from all over the US, from the federal government, and from several foreign governments as well.

❝ *The government allocates it [refined oil] and decides where it will go. . . . And that's why now, deeper in the south, in Florida right now and in California—believe it or not—the lines are beginning to form again in the gasoline stations. You know why? Because the federal agency . . . has forgotten that people in the south continue to drive as much in the winter as they do in the summer and the allocations are based on the idea that they would not drive as much based on the states in the northeast and the snow drifts and so forth that leave the car in the garage for a while.* **❞** (*Wash. Star,* 3/2/80)

A spokesman for the Department of Energy's Economic Regulatory Administration says no, gasoline allocation is not based on driving patterns of "states in the northeast." It is based on each state's drivers' use for the base year—summer and winter—of 1978.

❝ *What would I cut? . . . Right now the GAO has furnished the Congressional Budget Office with a list of 41 specific items.*

Q: "You are aware, I am sure, that the US has an utterly disgraceful number of murders. Do you believe that there's any correlation between the wide dissemination of guns in this country and this disgraceful record? And, in short, isn't it time for a truly effective gun control law?"

A: "We get back to the old argument again—and I have stated many times—you cannot find in the states, the various states that have gun control laws, that there is any proportionate difference in the crimes committed where there are those very strict laws and where they are far looser in their laws." (2/16/83)

Oh, yes you can. According to the 1981 FBI Uniform Crime Report, 63% of all homicides in the US are committed in the southern and western regions of the country, where handgun laws are the weakest.

80

NEWS ITEM

In Grand Island, Nebraska, Reagan asserted that one definition of the family then being used in Washington was "any two persons living together." Asked in Amarillo, Texas, to name the agency using that definition, he said that he did not know. No one else was able to come up with a government agency operating on such a definition, and none has stepped forward to claim the honor. (*New York Times*, 4/14/80)

FALSE ALARM ➡

All of them are totally unnecessary, spelled out right down to the penny . . . they total $11 billion [in savings], those 41 items. . . . 🙿 (*Wash. Star*, 3/2/80)

They totaled zero, those 41 items, at least as far as the Government Accounting and Congressional Budget offices are concerned—spokesmen for both said they knew of no such list.

🙶 *There's a useless layer of bureaucracy up on top of HEW. And it costs HEW three dollars in overhead to deliver one dollar to a needy person in this country.* 🙿 (CBS Network News, 4/3/80)

It cost 12 cents to deliver one dollar of health care.

🙶 *If you count the part of Alaska actually under the state's control, it's a smaller state than Rhode Island.* 🙿 (*New York Times*, 4/13/80)

A lot of Alaska *is* owned or controlled by the federal government, but not quite that much. Of Alaska's 586,412 square miles, about 80,000 are under state and private ownership. Rhode Island has 1,214 square miles all to itself.

🙶 *If the figures that I've been given are correct, in these last three years the federal government has increased by 131,000 [workers].* 🙿 (*Time*, 4/14/80)

The figures were not correct. The Bureau of Labor Statistics put the average number of federal workers in 1976 at 2,733,000 and in 1979 at 2,773,000—for a grand total increase of 40,000.

🙶 *Washington will be able to decide where you'll work, what kind of work you'll do, what you'll get paid, what you'll produce, and what the product will sell for.* **99** (*Wash. Post,* 4/23/80)

This description of the Humphrey-Hawkins Full Employment Bill is highly inflammatory. Neither the original legislation nor the compromise signed into law would do any such thing. The legislation prescribes the national goal of full employment, period.

66 *Up in Bellingham, Washington, HEW was threatening to take away the federal funds from the school district there, because they are spanking boys and girls in unequal numbers.* **99** (CBS Network News, 4/3/80)

Not quite. First of all, the school district was in Bellevue, not Bellingham. And the problem—at least as far as HEW was concerned—was discrimination against women in athletic facilities and vocational training. There did seem to be more cases of corporal punishment involving boys than girls, but HEW was not threatening to cut off funds for that reason.

66 *The government is actually making a sizable profit on that particular program [tobacco price supports].* **99** (*New York Times,* 5/1/80)

Reagan attempts to justify tobacco price supports despite his free-market philosophy. It doesn't work—according to tobacco specialists at the Department of Agriculture, the tobacco price supports cost the government in some years and make a little money in others, breaking even over the long run.

66 *Now last year [1979], the farmer's income—they talk about parity; I prefer to talk about net income, equity on their investment and on their equity—and actually their income pro-rated out to 90% of parity.* **99** (*New York Times,* 5/1/80)

66 *Property rights and freedom are inseparable. I believe that in a variety of ways, through environmental controls, through such things as OSHA, the government is trying to minimize the ownership of private property in this country.* **99** (*New Republic,* 5/24/80)

◀ LITTLE KNOWN FUN FACT

Talking to corngrowers in Des Moines, Iowa, in August 1982, the President said that a congressman "from the heart of our biggest city" was once assigned to the House Agriculture Committee and promptly proposed "that government should confiscate all food and divide it equally among all the people because food was a natural resource belonging to everyone." According to the White House Press Office, however, "the story was not true; the President intended it as a joke."

Parity is an index that attempts to relate the purchasing power of farmers today to their power at the beginning of the century. According to the *Times,* "Parity can be measured in different ways, but by all measures it was far below 90% last year."

66 *[The Department of Education] is planning all manner of things to limit and restrict institutions of this kind [St. Joseph's College in Philadelphia] because their faith is totally in public education.* 99 (*The New Yorker,* 9/29/80)

No one in the press or Reagan entourage was able to come up with any idea of what the candidate might have been talking about.

66 *The federal government did not create the states, the states created the federal government.* 99 (Inaugural address, 1/20/81)

The original 13 colonies did get together and create our constitutional system, including the federal government. Yet the federal government "created" the other 37 states. Their land was either bought with federal monies or won at war by federal armies. Of the 37 states admitted to our nation after ratification, only Texas chose to become part of the US while a sovereign entity. The federal government did, however, assume Texas' debt when it became a state.

66 *In England, if a criminal with a gun, even if he was arrested for burglary, or theft, or whatever he was doing, was tried for first degree murder and hung if he was found guilty.* 99 (4/15/82)

A *New York Times* search of English law going back to the 14th century failed to turn up this legal standard. A member of the Law Society in Britain pointed out that there had once been a law that punished by execution the use of a gun that led to death, but never merely the carrying of a gun. After the error was pointed out, Press Secretary Larry Speakes commented, "Well, it's a good story though. It made the point, didn't it?"

66 There is no relaxing of—in the field of antitrust or antimonopoly—on the part of our government at this time, nor will there be. 99 (5/14/82)

Three months earlier the Reagan administration tried to eliminate antitrust enforcement by the Federal Trade Commission over the following three years by cutting off funding for the FTC's Bureau of Competition. Congress refused.

66 [Alexis de Tocqueville said] 'You know, in America someone sees a problem that needs solving. And they cross the street and talk to a neighbor about it. And the first thing you know a committee is formed.' And he said, 'Finally, the problem is solved.' And he said, 'You won't believe this. But not a single bureaucrat had anything to do with it.' 99 (11/12/82)

When asked if de Tocqueville really mentioned the word "bureaucrat," a White House spokeswoman said, "The President changed it a little." The more familiar quotation: "If a stoppage occurs in a thoroughfare, and the circulation of the public is hindered, the neighbors immediately constitute a deliberative body and this extemporaneous assembly gives rise to an executive power which remedies the inconvenience before anybody has thought of recurring to an authority superior to that of the persons immediately concerned."

HUH???

Q: "Don't you think that things might have been different if Hinckley had had more difficulty in being able to get a gun?"

A: *"Sure would have been more comfortable, except that at two o'clock in the afternoon, thereabouts, out there surrounded by many of you, he did what he did in an area that has about the strictest gun control laws that there are in the US."* (2/16/83)

The only problem with the President's argument against strict gun control laws is that John Hinckley did not obtain his gun in strictly controlled Washington. Hinckley got his weapon at Rocky's Pawn Shop in Dallas, Texas, where all you have to do to get a gun is pay for it.

UNKINDEST CUTS
Reagan & Social Programs

When it comes to the circus act that is his economic program, Ronald Reagan is like the Flying Wallendas; he scorns the use of a safety net. Safety nets are for sissies, cheaters, and loafers—and if Reagan's taunting anecdotes over the years are any indication, that's exactly how he thinks of people on welfare. The poor exasperate Reagan for another reason; they aren't content with their lot. They should know they would be better off without those Great Society programs. And they should take it for granted that private charity will come to the rescue when the net is cut. They should, but for some reason they don't, and Reagan is hurt when people say he doesn't care about the poor; he was poor once himself, he says. But then, he was a Democrat once, too.

❝ *We were told four years ago that 17 million people went to bed hungry every night. Well, that was probably true. They were all on a diet.* **❞** (TV speech, 10/27/64)

❝ *. . . a faceless mass, waiting for hand-outs.* **❞** (Description of Medicaid recipients, 1965)

❝ *Today a newcomer to the state is automatically eligible for our many aid programs the moment he crosses the border.* **❞** (Speech announcing candidacy, 1/3/66)

The truth of the matter was that immigrants to California had to wait five years before becoming eligible for benefits. Reagan acknowledged his error, but nine months later said exactly the same thing.

❝ *Take the war on poverty—a matchless boondoggle, full of sound and fury, but still with no record of accomplishment to point to. . . . The latest is a multi-million-dollar scheme to set the Zuni Indians up in a cooperative store to retail their hand-craft jewelry. If it works (and the government says it will), they'll gross $150,000 a year. Overlooked is the pertinent fact the Zunis on their own are doing $2 million a year in the sale of their jewelry.* **❞** (Speech before Merchants and Manufacturers Assoc., 5/16/66)

Quite distorted. The federal government did give the Pueblo Indians of Zuni, New Mexico, a grant, but it was for $208,741—hardly a multi-million-dollar figure. And the tribe asked for a delay in the expenditure of the funds until they could construct a new building themselves to house the cooperative. As to the $2 million their jewelry sales grossed, the Indians themselves received only a small fraction of it.

66 *There's a woman in Chicago. She has 80 names, 30 addresses, 12 Social Security cards, and is collecting veteran's benefits on 4 non-existing deceased husbands. And she's collecting Social Security on her cards. She's got Medicaid, is getting food stamps, and she is collecting welfare under each of her names. Her tax-free cash income alone is over $150,000.* 99 (*New York Times*, 2/15/76)

The "Chicago Welfare Queen" got a lot of play during the 1976 Republican primary. Sometimes she had 12 names and 30 Social Security numbers, sometimes she was also an unwed mother on AFDC. Candidate Reagan never bothered to point out to his shocked small-town audiences that his story was largely allegation and rumor. The woman in question, Linda Taylor, had been officially charged with using 4 aliases—not 80—and fraudulent collection of $8,000—not $150,000. She had not, at the time of Reagan's statements, been convicted of anything.

66 *If you are a slum dweller, you can get an apartment with 11-foot ceilings, with a 20-foot balcony, a swimming pool and gymnasium, laundry room and play room, and the rent begins at $113.20 and that includes utilities.* 99 (*New York Times*, 2/15/76)

NEWS ITEM

Concerned with the costs of California's medical care to the elderly, Governor Reagan announced in July 1967, "Something must be done before this ill-conceived program bankrupts the state."

Yet, even though Governor Reagan gave four choices for the size of the upcoming Medi-Cal deficit ($210 million, $71 million, $51 million, and $60 million), not one of them ever showed up on the state's balance sheet. By August, the projected deficit was dropped from California budget projections; state revenues had paid for all Medi-Cal costs—without cuts in benefits or participants.

The Governor did not own up to the fact that the predicted deficit had never appeared until January 1968. (*L.A. Times*, 1/11/68)

HUH???

One day in the 1980 campaign, Reagan visited the Santa Marta Hospital in a Chicano area of East Los Angeles. He told the institution's staff that he had asked a nun there whether the hospital got "compensation from Medicaid or anything like that." According to the candidate, she answered "no." "I appreciate your pride in that," he told the group.

A "puzzled senior administrator" later informed reporters that 95% of the patients at Santa Marta were subsidized by either Medicaid or Medicare. (*Time*, 10/20/80)

Reagan based this statement on a project in East Harlem called Taino Towers. At the time, the coordinating director of the project, Robert Nichol, pointed out the following: only 92 of 656 units had 11-foot ceilings, and only over the kitchen and living space to save what would otherwise be wasted corridor space; there was no way anyone could get such an apartment for $113.20—the going rate was more like $450 or a quarter of the family's income; the pool and gym and other facilities mentioned were shared with the 200,000 people who lived in the community.

66 For more than 20 years the federal government has been building low cost housing for the poor. And they're constantly passing new programs, as each one fails. To date, the score is they have destroyed 3½ houses for every one they have built. 99 (*New York Times*, 6/27/76)

A statement apparently based on a decade-old study, by Reagan's economic adviser-to-be Martin Anderson, of the first federal urban program. The ratio seemed plausible, according to the Ford administration, only if applied exclusively to tracts that urban renewal marked for slum clearance—frequently in order to make way for commercial, not residential, development.

66 In North Carolina, in Gaston County, I found that they gave $21,000 to the county to buy heating oil for people who were too poor to heat their homes. Now they've discovered that $20,500 of that went for administrators' salaries and expenses to supervise the buying of $500 worth of oil. 99 (*New York Times*, 6/27/76)

Not quite. For bookkeeping purposes, part of the county's anti-poverty staff was listed in the emergency heating program.

Wayne Daves, director of Gaston Community Action, says this maneuver allowed the county to qualify for an additional federal grant of $11,300 that was used exclusively for fuel.

❝ *I never suggested that Social Security should be voluntary.* **❞** (*New York Times,* 9/17/80)

Not never. Voluntary Social Security was a staple of Reagan's mashed potato circuit speeches of the '60s. For example: "Social Security ought to be voluntary . . . so those who can make better provision for themselves are allowed to do so" (*Human Events,* Nov. 1966). Or, "Don't exchange freedom for the soup kitchen of compulsory insurance" (*New York Times,* 1/17/76).

❝ *Now, again this statement that somehow I wanted to destroy it and I just changed my tune, that I am for voluntary Social Security, which would mean the ruin of it. Mr. President, the voluntary thing that I suggested many years ago was that with a young man orphaned and raised by an aunt who died, his aunt was ineligible for Social Security insurance because she was not his mother. And I suggested that if this is an insurance program, certainly the person who is paying in should be able to name his own beneficiary. That is the closest I have ever come to anything voluntary with Social Security.* **❞** (Presidential debate, 10/28/80)

He has come a lot closer than that. See above.

❝ *There has been a great deal of misinformation and for that matter pure demagoguery on the subject of Social Security. . . .* **❞** (Radio address, 9/24/81)

The misinformation is on the subject of just how much the President wants to cut. He has acted to eliminate Social Secu-

NEWS ITEM

The President told a Republican audience in December 1981 about a woman in Illinois who supported CETA budget cuts even though her own job would be eliminated. He added, "She is now employed in a $25,000-a-year job in the private sector. She says it beats daytime television."

But according to *New York Times* reporter Howell Raines, Sue Long, the woman in question, left her job to go on the Illinois *state* payroll, and never made the daytime television remark.

88

NEWS ITEM

To highlight a mid-March 1982 speech on abuses of federal funds, the President said that Stuart F. Kindrick, Jr., who suffered brain damage and partial paralysis as a result of an industrial accident in 1973, had lost his Social Security disability benefits because he had been improperly drawing them while holding a job for three years.

Later, however, Social Security officials said they had no proof Kindrick ever worked and drew payments simultaneously. Indeed, shortly before Reagan's accusation, Social Security officials decided Kindrick was too crippled to work and sent him $2,324 for the months his status had been in question. "If I'm working, I'd like to know where so I can go and pick up my check," Kindrick said, obviously disgusted by the whole affair. (*Chicago Sun-Times*, 3/24/82)

rity benefits for students who are children of deceased and disabled workers; proposed cutting the minimum benefit for Social Security recipients; and allowed his Health and Human Services Secretary to propose cutting benefits at 62 years of age—a proposal rejected by the Senate, 95–0.

❝ *Once we get the private sector in the driver's seat, we can go just as far as your imagination and inspiration can take us. For example: Pima County, Arizona, concerned about the impact of budget cuts, looked into their hot meals program for the elderly. They discovered that out of their $53,000 budget, $50,000 went for staffing and administrative overhead. So, they eliminated the overhead, ran the program with volunteers. They doubled the food budget to $6,000, saved $47,000, and ended up feeding twice as many people.* ❞ (1/14/82)

Reagan's imagination took him pretty far on this one. "There's nothing been saved in overhead," said Frances Freeman, director of the South Park Area Council in Pima County. She added that the President "got his figures a little mixed up." Last year the council spent "between $7,000 and $8,000" on food, not the $3,000 the President implied. People were working for the program as volunteers rather than on salary because federal grant money had run out—they were waiting for new funds before going back on the payroll. The increase in the number of people fed resulted from the closure of other government-sponsored facilities.

❝ *In 20 years, the federal budget increased five-fold and the cost of welfare grew ten-fold. But that didn't help many local governments which lost effective control of their communities. It didn't help small businesses hit by the highest interest rates in a hundred years. It didn't help the working poor and pensioners flattened by double-digit inflation and taxation.* ❞ (1/14/82)

It probably did. The standard of living has doubled since 1960. Accounting for inflation, per capita disposable income, the average income after taxes, rose, in 1972 dollars, from $2,709 in 1960 to $4,472 in 1980. In 1959, 22.4% of Americans lived below the poverty line. By 1981, that figure had been cut nearly in half.

66 *There has not been a cut in the overall spending on human resources.* 99 (1/19/82)

Yes there has. While the total budget the President submitted for 1983 was $32 billion bigger than the 1982 budget, defense spending alone was up $33.6 billion for 1983, and interest payments on the national debt were up another $13.4 billion. Despite Reagan's assertion, total spending for everything else—including "human resources"—would go down under the Reagan budget.

66 *I don't believe that there is going to be any cut that's going to affect students with true need. . . .* 99 (2/18/82)

In fact, the needier the student, the harder he or she would be hit by Reagan's student-aid cuts. For example, a college student whose family is unable to make any contribution currently relies on an aid package that includes a maximum Pell Grant, a Supplement Grant, a work-study job, a State Student-Incentive Grant, and a Direct Loan or Guaranteed Loan. President Reagan's proposed program would reduce that student's Pell Grant, take away the Supplemental Grant and the State Grant, reduce the work-study award by 28%, make Direct Loans scarcer, and make Guaranteed Loans more expensive.

66 *We haven't touched Social Security.* 99 (3/31/82)

TALL TALE

During the 1982 election campaigns, a Republican TV advertisement showed a white-haired mailman delivering July's Social Security check, which contained an automatic cost-of-living increase in benefits. "President Reagan kept his promise to the American people," the ad proclaimed.

In fact, Reagan *opposed* the increase in Congress, which passed it anyway. Rep. Claude Pepper (D-Fla.), chairman of the House Committee on Aging, said that for Reagan to claim credit for the increase "lowers the art of deception to depths not explored since the Nixon administration." (*New York Times,* 7/7/82)

WISHFUL THINKING DEPT.

When Reagan made this statement, Congress had already approved his proposal to eliminate Social Security benefits for students who were children of deceased or disabled workers, and to end the minimum benefit for future beneficiaries.

DIPSY DOODLE ➤

❝I hear the downbeat talk about . . . hunger and so forth. There'll be two times as many food stamps as there were in 1978. The increase is that much.❞ (3/24/82)

The increase in *appropriations* is that much. But the price of food has increased 40% since 1978, and the average participation in the program has increased by 5.7 million people over the four-year period. According to the Congressional Budget Office, 5/6 of all households receiving food stamps will have their real benefits *reduced.*

TALL TALE ➤

❝A young man went into a grocery store and he had an orange in one hand and a bottle of vodka in the other, and he paid for the orange with food stamps and he took the change and paid for the vodka. That's what's wrong [with food stamps].❞ (Chicago Sun-Times, 3/26/82)

Let's get back to reality. According to Mary C. Jarratt, the assistant secretary of agriculture who oversees the food stamp program, change from food stamp transactions is limited to 99¢ in coin—hardly the price of vodka. Jarratt told a House nutrition subcommittee that such anecdotes, which she called examples in the extreme, "do not represent a constructive approach to the situation." She added, "We are following up on that with the White House . . . to find the source of the story."

❝About 3.4 million households will receive subsidized housing assistance at the beginning of 1983. By the end of 1985, under our proposals, 400,000 more households will be added to

the list. **"** (3/29/82)

The President neglected to add that the increase of 400,00 households was 300,000 less than the 700,000 proposed under Carter. Congress, however, did not pass all the proposed Reagan cuts, so by 1985 there were an estimated 4.1 million subsidized households.

" *We have found in the first investigation that 57% of the stores that were investigated are selling items for food stamps that are banned. . . .* **"** (*New York Times,* 4/1/82)

Quite misleading. The "investigation" was not based on a random sample. The USDA had "some reason to suspect a problem," according to USDA official John W. Bode, in all the stores investigated, which represented only 2% of the total number of stores in the program.

" *. . . in an editorial in a paper this morning . . . they said we had less money for vaccinations for children and therefore there was going to be more sickness and perhaps more child death. Well, what they didn't see was that we actually have more money in for that program than we've had for others.* **"** (*New York Times,* 4/1/82)

"They" didn't see it because the money wasn't there. In March 1981, Reagan proposed a $6 million reduction in the federal funds allotted to states for immunization. Six months later he requested an additional $2.2 million cut. Congress compromised on a $2.3 million cut—not an increase—in that program. With the cost of vaccines sharply on the rise, the number of children immunized will be sharply reduced—perhaps even cut in half by fiscal 1983.

" *In the same editorial they criticized the women, infant and*

NEWS ITEM

In a Saturday morning radio address in February 1983, Mr. Reagan had some harsh words for his critics, whom he described as "misery merchants" and "doom-and-gloom criers." To make everyone feel better, and prove just how wrong those critics were, he asserted that his administration was increasing spending in "the social safety net" by "almost one-fourth." This spending increase he characterized as "welfare, medical, nutrition, and housing assistance for our most needy citizens, plus compensation for the unemployed."

Try mostly compensation for the unemployed. Almost two-thirds of that reassuring increase in social spending was due to the rise in unemployment compensation costs resulting from the recession. As ever, actual spending for welfare and housing is

children nutrition program. And I'm sure at first glance they must have thought something had happened. It's been merged with another program and is in there at much greater money than it has ever had before. ?? (*New York Times*, 4/1/82)

Something *had* happened—Reagan's budget proposed a $200 million cut in nutrition funds. Edwin L. Dale, Jr., Office of Management and Budget spokesman, said, "The President possibly misspoke slightly on that one."

66 *There have only been smaller increases than some of our big spenders would have preferred. ??* (5/8/82)

66 *There have been no budget cuts. ??* (6/15/82)

Wrong. Reagan's own budget shows a $3.805 billion cut in spending earmarked for training, employment, and labor services. Federal spending will also be lower—by $3.695 billion—in 1983 than in 1982 for three major programs that help the poor: Aid to Families with Dependent Children; Medicaid; and food and nutrition assistance, including food stamps.

66 *The decrease in poverty I referred to earlier started in the 1950s. By the time the full weight of the Great Society programs was felt, economic progress for America's poor had come to a tragic halt. ??* (9/19/82)

In 1967, the Field Foundation testified before Congress on hunger in America: "Wherever we went and wherever we looked, we saw children in significant numbers who were hungry and sick." A decade later, the Field team retraced its 1967 steps and found "far fewer grossly malnourished people in this country. . . ." They concluded that food stamps and other federal nutrition programs, implemented or inspired by

Great Society legislation, had made the difference.

❝** The family at a poverty level, where they don't pay taxes, their income is more than $500 better off simply because of the decrease in inflation. **❞ (10/6/82)

Or $600, $472, $400, depending on the President's mood. According to the Center on Budget and Policy Priorities, purchasing power for families at the poverty line has not gone up. When cuts in benefits that previously went to these families are included, many of the working poor have, more likely, lost ground.

❝** The food stamp program alone had grown in 15 years from $65 million to $11.3 billion—an increase of more than 16,000%. **❞ (10/28/82)

Boy, that is a big increase. But . . . in Fiscal Year 1966, over 2,700 counties, or nearly 90% of all counties in the United States, did *not* participate in the food stamp program. The program did not become nationwide until 1974. Comparing 1966 and 1981 expenditures is like comparing an embryo with a fully grown adult.

❝** For example, you mention nutrition. Well, right now in our budget we will be providing for about a 12% increase in the people that are eligible for the nutritional programs over what they knew in 1980. **❞ (2/16/83)

The budget in question provided for 100,000 *fewer* recipients of WIC (Women, Infant and Children) nutrition aid in 1984 than it did in 1980, according to the Center for Budget and Policy Priorities.

***❝** Now, some people I've seen have suddenly seized upon a*

NEWS ITEM CONT.
down since 1981, and will continue to go down under current administration proposals. In the same speech, the President quoted Abraham Lincoln: "Truth is generally the best vindication against slander." And so it is.
(*New York Times,* 2/16/83)

◀ **FALSE ALARM**

◀ **DIPSY DOODLE**

◀ **DIPSY DOODLE**

figure that has to do with school lunches, and they've said, 'Ah, there's a reduction in the number of school lunches.' Yes, there is, because for one thing there's a reduction in the number of children in school. . . . Maybe the baby boom is over, but suddenly their enrollment has dropped. 99 (2/9/83)

The 1.5% drop in public school enrollment from 1981 to 1982 does not come close to accounting for the 12% reduction in the number of students in the school lunch program. Many schools were forced to drop out of the program in 1982 because federal reimbursement was drastically cut and the schools could not carry the cost. In all, more than 3 million children were cut from the federal school lunch program.

LITTLE KNOWN FUN FACT ➤

66 *There haven't been cutbacks in funding for public educa-tion.* 99 (5/23/83)

Reagan's own budget figures show there have been. Federal outlays declined by $.2 billion in fiscal 1982. There was a further $.1 billion cut in fiscal 1983. When asked to justify the President's statement, a White House official said, "He doesn't believe there has been."

The Good Old Days

The Great Depression. Does Ronald Reagan have any idea what was really going on in this country in the 1930s? Riots, unrest, misery, discrimination, hopelessness—according to him, they never happened. FDR and the New Deal? Creeping fascism. Sure Reagan likes to quote Roosevelt—the man could make a speech—but that doesn't mean he likes FDR's ideas. Remember—while Reagan is piously invoking one of America's best-loved presidents, Reagan administration policy is steadily dismantling the programs FDR believed in.

"*Anyone who wants to take a look at the writings of the members of the brain trust of the New Deal will find that President Roosevelt's advisers admired the fascist system.* **"** (*New York Times,* 8/17/80)

Some of the New Dealers made references to the efficiency of the Italian government. So did Winston Churchill. This does not add up to an admiration for fascism. Neither FDR nor the New Deal brain trust ever hinted at adopting that political program.

" *Many of the New Dealers actually espoused what has become an epithet—fascism. . . . Ickes, [Secretary of the Interior] Harold Ickes, in his book, said that what we were striving for was a kind of modified form of communism.* **"** (*New York Times,* 12/23/81)

A White House spokeswoman said, "I don't know and can't find who he was referring to specifically." Arthur Schlesinger, Jr., who has read the Ickes diaries word for word, said there was nothing in them to substantiate such a charge.

" *Fascism was really the basis for the New Deal. It was Mussolini's success in Italy, with his government-directed economy, that led the early New Dealers to say, "But Mussolini keeps the trains running on time.* **"**
(*Time,* 5/17/76)

❝ I've always thought my father, God rest his soul, had the common sense that he would know that temporary fixes wouldn't work. ❞ (12/23/82)

Reagan made this comment in response to a reporter's question about what his own parents would have thought of a $5 billion public works program. The reason the reporter asked the question was that Reagan's father had been in charge of the WPA program in Dixon, Illinois. The President's answer directly contradicted his own 1965 autobiography, *Where's the Rest of Me?*: "There were no boondoggles in Dixon to speak of under the WPA; parks were created out of brush and swamp riverbeds, bridges over the river, and even a hangar at the new airport. Practically all the unemployed were able-bodied and capable, and they besieged him [Jack Reagan] for chances at working for their keep."

❝ Roosevelt at one time made a statement that the federal government had to get out of the business of—we didn't call it 'welfare' then, we called it 'relief' . . . . As he explained, the federal government was not the proper agency for that. ❞ (*New Republic,* 5/23/83)

After concluding that the federal government should "quit the business of relief," FDR, at the same time, went on to call for a federal program for those out of work that would replace relief with employment by means of the biggest peacetime appropriations ever.

❝ I didn't desert my party. It deserted me. I looked up FDR's old platform, and I discovered that it called for a restoration of states' rights and a reduction in the national budget. . . . The Roosevelt that I voted for had promised to cut federal spending

by 25%, had promised to return to the states and local communities authority and autonomy that had been unjustly seized by the federal government. **??** (*The New Republic*, 5/23/83)

Roosevelt made the promise of slashing government spending and reducing federal influence in 1932. Reagan voted for FDR not only in 1932, but also in 1936, 1940, and 1944. "Indeed," said William E. Leuchtenburg, author of *In the Shadow of FDR: From Harry Truman to Ronald Reagan,* "Reagan's devotion to Roosevelt was greatest *after* he had put through the precedent-smashing legislation that centralized authority in Washington."

?? *In the Great Depression, nothing like that [riots caused by economic hardship] ever took place when the situation was much worse. . . .* **??** (1/5/83)

Some incidents the President may have forgotten: Farmers in his native midwest sabotaged milk deliveries and food shipments, and stood by with shotguns to keep their homes from being foreclosed. Army troops brutally dispersed WW I veterans marching for a bonus in 1932. During the coal strikes in many states, police and sometimes state militia and the national guard arrested those "banding and confederating." Hundreds of mounted police stormed demonstrating auto workers in Detroit. Grocery stores in Oklahoma were raided during the food riots there. Ah, yes, those were the days.

KILLER TREES
Reagan & the Environment

Look at it this way. If trees cause pollution, then what do we need a Clean Air Act for? We know where those killers are located, and so does James Watt. That must be why he's so eager to sell off sections of the National Park System to lumber companies—then you'd see those pollution indexes plummet. You may think this is a joke, but Ronald Reagan doesn't. He's out on the ramparts, beating back "snail darters" and other "extreme environmentalists" who won't be happy until the White House looks like a bird's nest. They're a wily lot, those environmentalists, forever trying to pin dead fish on big business. But it doesn't have to be this way. With the cooperation of the EPA (if only the US Congress would get out of its way) and the Department of the Interior (headed by James Watt, a man you can trust), Ronald Reagan is going to see that this country is made safe once again for the toxic-waste-dumping habits of huge corporations. As for an environment safe for the rest of us—well, don't hold your breath.

❝ *They [the federal government] are making it impossible for the people to have any access or enjoyment from [public] lands, unless, maybe, you're a backpacker who gets on them yourself.* **❞** (*Field & Stream*, 10/80)

❝ *Swarms of locusts and grasshoppers; a plague of crickets, cutworms, and ants; and swarms of mosquitoes are making life miserable and even impossible in some parts of the world. . . . Some experts are treating this as an unexplainable mystery. Actually, there is no mystery about it. . . . The most effective pesticide, DDT, was outlawed . . . on the theoretical grounds that it might, under some circumstances, some day, harm someone or something.* **❞** (Radio, Oct. 1978)

DDT's most prized characteristic, the ability to linger in the environment and to provide long-term effects, ultimately backfires, since insects develop resistance to it. Meanwhile, the rest of us are slowly poisoned as it builds up in the food chain. By 1972, DDT had been detected in 99% of human tissue samples taken in the US. It is a proven carcinogen. It has a devastating effect on birds, fish, and other wildlife. That's why the EPA banned its use in this country.

FALSE ALARM

❝ The world is experiencing a resurgence of deadly diseases spread by insects because pesticides such as DDT have been prematurely outlawed. ❞ (Chicago Tribune, 5/10/80)

Nice try. Just because DDT's use is largely banned in this country doesn't mean it can't be manufactured here and sprayed elsewhere. In fact, the US exports more than 40 *million* pounds of DDT every year.

LITTLE KNOWN FUN FACT

❝ Approximately 80% of our air pollution stems from hydrocarbons released by vegetation, so let's not go overboard in setting and enforcing tough emission standards from man-made sources. ❞ (Sierra, 9/10/80)

Talk about the commonsense gap. Trees do emit hydrocarbons, but the EPA does not find that cause for concern. Trees decay into nitrous oxide, which is not an immediate threat to human health. On the other hand, the EPA projects that emissions of man-made oxides of nitrogen—which are harmful and which those "tough emission standards are intended to control—will increase by 50% by the year 2000.

WHAT A DIFFERENCE A DAY MAKES
4/17/67:
"I believe our country can and should have a Redwood National Park in California."

4/18/67:
". . . [T]here can be no proof given that a national park is necessary to preserve the redwoods. The state of California has already maintained a great conservation program."

❝ I know Teddy Kennedy had fun at the Democratic convention when he said that I had said that trees and vegetation cause 80% of the air pollution in this country. Well, he was a little wrong about what I said. First of all, I didn't say 80%, I said 92%, 93%, pardon me. And I didn't say air pollution, I said oxides of nitrogen. And I am right. Growing and decaying vegetation in this land are responsible for 93% of the oxides of nitrogen. ❞ (L.A. Times, 10/9/80)

The gap becomes the Grand Canyon. According to Dr. Michael

"Air pollution has been substantially controlled."
(Press release, 10/8/80)

"I don't think I've said anything of the kind."
(Oct. 9, *Time,* 10/20/80)

"Isn't it substantially under control? I think it is." (*Time,* 10/20/80)

Oppenheimer of the Environmental Defense Fund, industrial sources are responsible for at least 65% and possibly as much as 90% of the oxides of nitrogen in the US.

❝ *I have flown twice over Mt. St. Helens. I'm not a scientist and I don't know the figures, but I have a suspicion that one little mountain out there, in these last several months, has probably released more sulfur dioxide into the atmosphere than has been released in the last ten years of automobile driving or things of that kind.* ❞ (*Time,* 10/20/80)

Not even close. Automobiles are not regulated for sulfur dioxide, since they emit very little of it—although, at 81,000 tons a day, they are still beating out the "little mountain" 's peak activity of 2,000 tons a day. Utilities, which *are* regulated for sulfur dioxide, have managed to generate 200 million tons of the stuff in the last decade, or 50 times the volcano's total output of 4,000,000 tons. No contest.

❝ *As governor of California, I took charge of passing the strictest air pollution laws in the United States—the strictest air quality law that has ever been accepted.* ❞ (Presidential debate, 10/28/80)

Dead wrong. It was under Governor Pat Brown, who preceded Reagan in office, that California adopted the toughest anti-pollution measures in the nation. Reagan did put his name to some air and water quality legislation, but only under the most intense pressure from California environmentalists. The record shows that during his eight-year reign as Governor, Reagan worked to undermine and weaken environmental standards. *California Journal* reported that by 1973 the Air Resources Board had "faded from national prominence into a strange kind of bureaucratic malaise, in which it inhibits rather than aids the smog-control effort." Shades of EPA present?

" *Why hasn't anyone mentioned that in response to that [a Sierra Club petition calling for the dismissal of Interior Secretary Watt], a petition of over seven million signatures was brought in wanting him retained?* **"** (1/21/82)

Probably because that petition never got seven million signatures. White House officials didn't know where Reagan got the figure, and Secretary Watt's office could only turn up a small article in the *Casper Star-Tribune* where Marlene Simons of Outdoors Unlimited—a national organization promoting multiple land use—reported the still-unbelievable sum of four million signatures. But Douglas Scott, who directed the Sierra Club's petition drive against Watt, says the Outdoors Unlimited petition claimed as signatures endorsements by organizations. For example, if the Farm Bureau endorsed the petition, they claimed the Bureau's entire membership as signatories. Scott estimated the real take as more like 100,000, while "nobody's in doubt about our 1.1 million signatures. Outdoors Unlimited cannot tell us where their petitions are."

" *The maintenance of a free, essentially self-governing scientific community is one of the great strengths of our nation. To undermine this tradition by requiring that the EPA Science Advisory Board wear the label "industry" or "labor" or "consumer" is a modern-day version of Lysenkoism to which I must strongly object.* **"** (Presidential veto, 10/22/82)

Webster's New World Dictionary defines Lysenkoism as "a repudiated doctrine that characteristics acquired through environmental changes can be transmitted by heredity." White House spokesmen were "not sure" what the President meant by the comparison.

" *Now there are 23 settlements [of hazardous waste dumping cases] so far that I know of.* **"** (2/16/83)

PROS & CONS:

REDWOODS

"A tree's a tree. How many more do you need to look at?" (Sacramento *Bee,* 3/12/66)

". . . 115,000 acres of trees in the state park system is a lot to look at. How long can you look?" (Sacramento *Bee,* 4/28/66)

"I'm a fellow who bleeds every time a tree is cut down." (Fresno *Bee,* 4/28/66)

"I don't believe a tree is a tree and if you've seen one you've seem them all." (Sacramento *Bee,* 9/14/66)

"I just didn't say it." (Associated Press, 10/5/66)

WISHFUL THINKING DEPT.

DEPT. OF RETRACTIONS

On November 30, 1982, President Reagan invoked executive privilege to prevent Congress from reviewing subpoenaed EPA documents. On February 16, 1983, the President apparently switched course. In a nationally televised news conference, he said that his administration "will never invoke executive privilege to cover up wrongdoing." He added, "I can no longer insist on executive privilege if there's a suspicion in the minds of the people that maybe it is being used to cover some wrongdoing."

The very next day presidential spokesman Larry Speakes insisted that Reagan had not said what everybody thought he had. Rather, the records would be submitted to the Justice Department, which would then decide whether it was "necessary" to hand them over to Congress.

That's 21 more settlements than the EPA knows of.

❝ *And so I have ordered a complete investigation by the Justice Department into every charge [of mismanagement and political manipulation of the Superfund at EPA] that is made.* ❞ (2/16/83)

Not as far as Richard Hauser, a deputy to White House counsel Fred F. Fielding, was concerned. Asked by reporters about the President's statement, he admitted that the Justice Department investigation did not deal with mismanagement and that, if the political manipulation did not amount to criminal acts, "that would be the end of it as far as the Justice Department is concerned."

❝ *There is today in the United States as much forest as there was when Washington was at Valley Forge.* ❞ (3/5/83)

Not even in the ball park, Mr. President—the amount of forest land in the United States has dropped significantly since George first wielded his ax. According to the US Forest Service, only about 30% of the 736.6 million acres of forest land that existed in 1775 still exists today.

❝ *I will match this administration's record with regard to environmental matters against that of any other administration. And we have been far more successful. We're spending more money on parks and on acquisition of parks and so forth than the previous administration had spent in all its four years, in these two years so far.* ❞ (3/29/83)

Off by $1.4 billion. President Carter's four budgets for parks totaled $2.9 billion, according to Interior Department records. By the end of 1983, Reagan's budget came to $1.5 billion.

SHORTAGE OF SENSE
Reagan & Energy Policy

Like an honest welfare recipient or a nuclear freeze movement free of Soviet agents, the idea of an energy shortage leaves Ronald Reagan baffled. After all, the President's America-first policy dictates a US reserve of oil larger than any other on earth. But that honor, despite our best efforts, stays with the Saudis. So maybe we could dismantle government regulation and the price system and still solve those energy problems. Problems such as aging transit and factory systems that waste fuel. Or oil prices that drop so much the oil men won't spend money finding hard-to-reach reserves. Or nuclear plants so costly and unreliable that the promise of abundant energy is the only thing cheap about them. The energy crisis, in short, is one of those national headaches with a long history and complicated origins. You could never tell that by the Reagan prescription: Take two aspirin, and leave on all the lights!

❝As for radiation, a coal-fired plant emits more radiation than a nuclear-powered plant. You even get more from watching TV or having your teeth X-rayed.❞ (Radio, Nov. 1978)

False, according to Dr. Ernest Sternglass of the University of Pittsburgh. Coal-fired plants do not emit iodine or strontium-90 or cesium—dangerous sources of radioactivity that accumulate in vital organs such as the thyroid gland. Nor do TV sets or dental X-rays. Total radiation to organs is hundreds of times greater from a nuclear plant than from any of these sources. Moreover, federal law limits color TVs to emitting 0.05 millirems/hour at the screen itself—in other words, 1/10,000 of the federal radiation exposure limit (0.5 rems) for nuclear power plant operation.

❝It takes 12 years to get a nuclear power plant built in Amer-

TALL TALE

"The truth is, all of the nuclear waste now on hand and yet to be accumulated between now and the year 2000, could be stacked on a single football field and the stack would only be six feet high." (Radio, Nov. 1978)

"The waste from one nuclear power plant in a year would take less storage space than a dining room table." (Radio, Apr. 1979)

"All the waste in a year from a nuclear power plant could be stored under a desk." (*Burlington* [Vt.] *Free Press*, 2/15/80)

These strange myths were exploded by Marvin Resnikoff in a July/August 1980 *Sierra* magazine article. The football field estimate is closest to reality— although only for a single plant's wastes for a single year of operation. The football field would also

ica. It only takes four or five in most other countries. The seven or eight years' difference is not construction time in our country; it is paperwork and the multitudinous permits required by the government. **"** (Radio, Apr. 1979)

Wrong again. It does take ten to twelve years to build a nuclear power plant in the US, but that puts us ahead of India, Spain, Italy, and Britain, and behind Japan and France. In fact, the only country to do it in four years is Japan—once. As for the charge of regulatory sabotage, a congressional report concludes these claims "have been grossly exaggerated." The reasons for the French and Japanese lead are more logistical than bureaucratic. The Japanese work on their reactors around the clock, and the French have maximized efficiency by standardizing design.

" *Incidentally, the total radioactivity the people and the animals were exposed to in the immediate vicinity of the plant [Three Mile Island] was less than the difference between living in Dallas or living in the higher altitudes of Denver, Colorado.* **"** (Radio, May 1979)

Reagan is again omitting the most important aspect of radiation, the internal dose to critical organs. This internal dose, which comes from breathing iodine in the air, drinking locally produced milk and the local water, etc., is about 100 times as much as the 70-millirem average difference between Dallas and Denver.

" *To put things in focus, Dr. Alvin Weinberg of Oak Ridge [National Laboratories] brought a Geiger counter to a committee room of the US Senate. It registered higher radiation than escaped at Three Mile Island.* **"** (Radio, Aug. 1979)

Dr. Weinberg found the last sentence of the Reagan statement "difficult to interpret." He did in fact take a Geiger counter into a Senate committee room, and it did register five times the radioactivity that he had measured as "background" radiation at Atlanta Airport. While newspaper accounts of Three Mile Island radioactivity suggested that radiation levels were only two to three times "background," Weinberg believes that levels were probably much higher immediately after the accident. In any case, Weinberg's comparison applies only to gamma radiation and does not take into account the most dangerous forms of radioactivity—iodine, strontium-90, and cesium—which Senate committee walls do not emit.

66 *[Oil industry profits] were well below the average profit level of the rest of business and industry in America.* 99 (Ripon Forum, Oct. 1979)

Between 1974 and 1979, earnings per share for American oil and gas companies increased an average of 17.3%; for all industry the average increase was 12.6%. Other yardsticks of profitability—return on equity, return on total capital—put the oil industry either on a par with or slightly below, not well below, industry averages.

66 *What's wrong with adding a realistic energy policy in which we recognize the fact that right here in our own country we have the potential for the energy sources that we're presently importing?* 99 (*New York Times*, 1/2/80)

What's wrong is it's not realistic. Although American oil companies have stepped up drilling in the United States, they are beginning to wonder how sensible that policy is. Since the Prudhoe Bay discovery in the early '70s, no major tract of new oil wealth has been discovered in the US, and domestic reserves are steadily declining despite intense exploration.

TALL TALE CONT.

have to be underground, way underground. And it would not accommodate *all* the nuclear waste from the operation of a plant but only the *high-level* waste. A single nuclear plant's annual high-level waste might fit under your dining room table, but you wouldn't be able to go into the dining room—the waste would be generating too much heat and radioactivity. For those reasons, high-level waste has to be separated into small portions and spaced apart in a deep underground repository—no such repository has yet been sited or constructed. *All* the wastes from the nuclear energy process—including the remains from mining and milling uranium, low-level wastes from plant operation, the used plants themselves—would fill many, many football fields and still not be safely stored.

Whichever way you slice it, the US must continue to depend on the Arab states for much of its oil.

WISHFUL THINKING DEPT. ▶

66 We have more oil and gas yet to be found in America than we have used so far. 99 (*New York Times*, 3/29/80)

Not really. The Department of Energy estimates that a total of 460 billion barrels of oil have been discovered in the US since 1867. Of that figure, 121 billion have been produced, and with today's technology we can get at 27 billion more. Recovery techniques still in the laboratory might be able to extract another 18–53 billion. That leaves 259 billion no one knows how to reach. As for natural gas—we've consumed about 650 trillion cubic feet since 1946. We have 201 trillion cubic feet to go.

66 Right now, we have seven plants, seven nuclear plants that are finished, completed . . . and yet they can't go on line producing electricity. They have not yet been able to get a license and the government go-ahead to do that. If they did go on line, instantly they would save us 700,000 barrels of oil a year. No, wait a minute, a day. 99 (*Wash. Star*, 3/2/80)

Only four of the seven plants were ready for licensing at the time, according to the Atomic Energy Forum, the industry's leading trade association. Utility owners of six of these plants estimated that, together, they would stop buying a total of 100,000 barrels—not 700,000—a day. The owner of the seventh uses coal rather than oil to power his electrical system.

LITTLE KNOWN FUN FACT ▶

66 I've said it before and I'll say it again. The US Geological Survey has told me that the proven potential for oil in Alaska alone is greater than the proven reserves in Saudi Arabia. 99 (*Detroit Free Press*, 3/23/80)

No matter how many times he's said it, it's wrong. According to the USGS, the Saudi reserves of 165.5 billion barrels are *17 times* the proven reserves—9.2 billion barrels—in Alaska.

66 *The windfall profits tax would cost one million barrels in the US a day in lost production in the first year.* 99 *(Time,* 4/14/80)

According to the US government estimate cited by *Time* magazine, the tax would cost 100,000 barrels a day, or a tenth of the Reagan estimate.

66 *Trains are not any more energy efficient than the average automobile, with both getting about 48 passenger miles to the gallon.* 99 *(Chicago Tribune,* 5/10/80)

The US Department of Transportation figures that a 14-car train traveling at 80 mph gets 400 passenger miles to the gallon. A 1980 auto with good mileage carrying an average of 2.2 people gets 42.6 passenger miles to the gallon.

66 *Nuclear power is the cleanest, the most efficient, and the most economical energy source, with no environmental problems.* 99 *(Sierra,* 9/10/80)

Cleanest? The entire nuclear fuel chain emits carcinogenic radiation, much more so than coal, although coal also is dirty. Wind and solar power are much cleaner, as is the most cost-effective "source" of energy, conservation.

Most efficient? The losses from electrical generation are large, since only a fraction of the thermal energy of a plant is converted into electricity, and more is lost in transmission. Natural gas, for example, is much more efficient.

Most economical? Nuclear costs more than coal, and much more than conservation, which can save a kilowatt-hour cheaper

66 *It would be wonderful eventually, but the technology is such that right now, to equal the power output we are getting from nuclear generators, we would have to cover the entire state of New York with mirrors. I don't think the environmentalists would hold still for that.* 99 *(Field & Stream,* Oct. 1980)

◄ WISHFUL THINKING DEPT.

than it costs to make an additional kilowatt-hour.

No environmental problems? This is an incredible statement. There are problems with the disposal of radioactive mill tailings and radioactive waste. There are problems connected with continuous emissions of low levels of radiation. There are thermal pollution problems associated with warming bodies of water that are being used as plant coolant. And there is the "environmental" problem of nuclear war, which nuclear power makes more likely by making available necessary techniques, trained personnel, and fissionable materials to a number of countries that may not always have the best interests of the US uppermost in their minds.

DIPSY DOODLE ➤

66 *Government regulations and production barriers are the two chief causes of the energy crisis we are in.* 99 (*Science*, 10/10/80)

Try OPEC as a factor, and you get a clearer picture of the source of the energy crisis. In 1972, just before the first Arab oil emergency, the US devoted some 2% of its GNP to energy costs. In 1980, after the price of Saudi crude rose 750% in constant dollars, the country had to spend 8% of the GNP on energy. As for production barriers, when Congress dismantled most of them after 1973, the oil companies began to drill with a will, and oil and gas wells in Louisiana and along the Gulf began to dry up. Sometimes the oil isn't there even if you want it to be.

66 *We have a profound responsibility that as we go forward with nuclear power, we must do it on the basis of every precaution for safety that can be taken.* 99 (2/19/82)

While Reagan advocates caution, his administration throws it to the winds. For instance, there is a push to speed up licensing of nuclear power plants; the most dangerous aspects of nuclear power are being promoted, including lifting Carter's ban on commercial reprocessing of spent fuel (despite lack of industry interest) and pushing the controversial breeder reactor; funds for alternative energy sources are being cut; delays are allowed in the implementation of safety procedures identified as a result of the Three Mile Island accident; backfitting of existing nuclear plants with new safety equipment is not being required of plants with relatively good records although their equipment is just as likely to wear out as plants that don't have good records; and finally, the administration proposes that the right of the public to participate in licensing be drastically curtailed.

THERE OUGHTA NOT BE A LAW
Reagan & Justice

What Ronald Reagan really doesn't like about our legal system is that, after many a fit and start, it often works the way it should. Blacks and whites protest against racial injustice; Congress and the courts, after much prodding, move to correct it. Legislators debate the legality of American aid to anti-Sandinista forces; the Boland Amendment defines what the government can and cannot do. Rules of evidence evolve to protect due process—but rarely prevent officers from making an arrest. Courts and Congress, lawyers and litigants, shake out the complex issues. Of course, Ronald Reagan and complexity go together like oil and vinegar. In *his* march of progress he'd much prefer a judicial lockstep, where presidential orations and Moral Majority invocations prevail: viz., the Supreme Court ban on school prayer is overturned; there is no affirmative action; former officials cannot publish uncensored memoirs; and the Legal Services Corporation stops operating. Ronald Reagan does want to guarantee our liberties, but he may not understand that he isn't the only one who gets to define them. Has he ever read the Freedom of Information Act? The Bill of Rights? The Constitution? Do you really want to know?

❝ *[The Rumford 'open housing' Act] was introduced into the Legislature in the last six minutes of the 1963 session . . . and was forced through hastily and without proper consideration.* **❞** (Speech, California Real Estate Assoc., 10/30/66)

The Rumford Act—designed to prevent discrimination in the sale of federally subsidized housing—was introduced early in the 1963 session, was the subject of extensive committee hearings, and was finally passed in the closing minutes of the session.

❝ *. . . first of all—the Hatch Act, there are some fifteen million*

111

public employees in the United States. If you grant each one of them only influence over one additional vote, such as a family member, you are talking about a voting bloc of 30 million people who conceivably can have any number of conflicts of interest. . . . (NBC "Meet the Press," 5/1/77)

First of all, that voting bloc already exists. The Hatch Act, which prohibits federal employees from participating in political campaigns, does not prevent them from influencing the votes of their immediate family.

For many years the United Nations has had before it two covenants, the Covenant on Civil and Political Rights and the United Nations Covenant on Economic, Social, and Cultural Rights. Both specifically omit the right to own property or to be protected from arbitrary seizure without compensation. . . . What is apparently little known by the American people is that President Carter has signed both of these United Nations covenants which, in effect, nullify the inalienable right of an individual to own property—if they are ratified by the United States Senate, United Nations treaties become laws of the land, superceding all other laws. (Radio, Mar. 1978)

This is utter nonsense. Property rights are protected under the fourth, fifth, and fourteenth amendments to the US Constitution. A treaty or covenant that does not specifically take these rights away, as neither of these do, leaves those amendments fully in force. Besides, it is hardly logical that peanut baron Carter would have signed anything nullifying the right to own property.

[The United States Supreme Court is guilty of] an abuse of power as bad as the transgressions of Watergate and the bribery on Capitol Hill. (New York Times, 2/22/80)

It doesn't do good to open doors for someone who doesn't have the price to get in. If he has the price, he may not need the laws. There is no law saying the Negro has to live in Harlem or Watts. (San Francisco Chronicle, 9/9/67)

The Court's "crime": to let federal abortion funding to poor women continue while it reviewed the power of Congress to cut off those funds.

LITTLE KNOWN FUN FACT ▶

66 [John Marshall] wasn't even a lawyer. 99 (Presidential debate, 3/13/80)

The great Chief Justice of the US Supreme Court received his law license in 1780 and set up practice in 1783. According to Reagan aide Martin Anderson, Reagan meant to say that Marshall never went to law school, since his formal training was a matter of a few lectures at the College of William & Mary. Anderson: "He says it wrong. That's all."

TALL TALE ▶

66 Mrs. Brown took this all the way to the Supreme Court because of her own memories of her childhood when she had to go miles past a school near her home simply because of segregation. And then she had a daughter of her own, and Mrs. Brown is opposed to busing in her own community because, she said, now her daughter is bused miles past tne school near their home, and she said that wasn't what she had in mind. 99 (10/4/82)

Reagan's attempt to use Linda Brown Smith of *Brown* v. *Board of Education* to support his administration's anti-busing policy finds him once again at odds with reality. First, Linda Brown Smith's daughter recently graduated from the public high school two blocks from her home—Topeka doesn't bus children for racial balance. Second, Smith asked a federal judge to reopen her case because, she contended, her daughter was still the victim of *de facto* segregation in the Topeka school system. Third, Mrs. Smith's last public statement on the issue was pro-busing. On NBC's "Today," she told Phil Donahue, "I know what it is to have to get up early and go catch a bus in the cold and ride clear across town. But I also say if

NEWS ITEM

In reply to a reporter's question at a Charlotte, N.C., news conference, Ronald Reagan said that the sit-in demonstrations waged by southern blacks in the '60s to gain access to public accommodations were wrong because they violated the law and the rights of others. (*New York Times*, 11/21/75)

this is the solution, for now we should have busing."

" The First Amendment doesn't say anything about that [prayer in schools]. " (10/17/81)

It does, at least according to the Supreme Court of the United States. The Court ruled, in *Engle* v. *Vitale*: "Under that amendment's prohibition against governmental establishment of religion, as reinforced by the provisions of the 14th Amendment, government in this country, be it state or federal, is without power to prescribe by law any particular form of prayer which is to be used as an official prayer in carrying on any program of governmentally sponsored religious activity."

" If a policeman stops a car for a traffic violation and finds a sack of dope on the seat of the car, under the present case law, they can't introduce that—he can't arrest that man for a dope violation and use that dope as evidence because he stopped the man for a traffic violation. " (1/27/82)

Certainly he can. As long as the policeman was stopping the car for a legitimate reason in the first place (a traffic violation is a legitimate reason) and as long as the sack of dope was "in plain view," the arrest is valid and the dope can be introduced as evidence.

" There's a law by which things of this kind [clandestine intelligence operations] have to be cleared with congressional committees before anything is done. . . . " (2/18/82)

Not quite. The Intelligence Oversight Act of 1980 gives select intelligence committees of the Senate and the House the right to be *informed* of covert intelligence operations. They do not "clear" such operations—they have no veto power. The President may, in fact, delay notification—in some circum-

DEPT. OF RETRACTIONS

At a question and answer session with reporters, Reagan was asked whether he believed the *Weber* decision—which allowed firms to conduct voluntary affirmative action programs—should be overturned. He replied: "Well, if this [decision] is something that simply allows the training and the bringing up so there are more opportunities for them in voluntary agreement between the union and management, I can't see any fault with that. I'm for that." (12/17/81) Maybe he is, but his administration isn't. Assistant Attorney General William Bradford Reynolds has repeatedly emphasized that the administration's position is that it is illegal and unconstitutional to give preference to any group of people. The White House later retracted the President's remarks.

❝ *I am eternally optimistic, and I happen to believe that we've made great progress from the days when I was young and this country didn't even know it had a racial problem.* ❞ (Presidential debate, 10/28/80)

DIPSY DOODLE ➤

stances—until the operation is completed.

❝ *The Constitution says . . . 'The right of the people to keep and bear arms, shall not be infringed.'* ❞ (Speech before National Rifle Association, 5/16/82)

The full text of the Second Amendment reads: "A well regulated militia being necessary to the security of a free State, the right of the people to keep and bear arms shall not be infringed." The language Reagan omitted, the Supreme Court has decreed, means that the military and the police can carry arms, but that there is no constitutional right for citizens to bear arms.

❝ *There are so few of those [finishing or preparatory] schools, compared to the general parochial schools, throughout the country. But in this survey of 54 schools, they found 56% in those parochial schools were black.* ❞ (9/14/82)

Defending his plan to give tuition tax credits to families with children in independent schools forces the President to overlook the big picture. According to the US Census Bureau (1975), there are 8.5 white families for every black family in the US, and there are 17.8 white families with a child in a non-public school for every black family. So a white child is twice as likely to go to a non-public school as a black child.

❝ *The Justice Department has filed nine new anti-discrimination cases against public employers and has reviewed more than 9,000 electoral changes to determine compliance with the Voting Rights Act. And that, too, is a higher level of activity than in any prior administration.* ❞ (9/15/82)

The 9,000 reviews Reagan mentioned were those required each time a state or local government covered by the Voting

Rights Act made a change in its election law, according to a report by the independent Washington Council of Lawyers. Such automatic reviews have been particularly numerous in the wake of the 1980 census that forced widespread redistricting. The Reagan administration filed only two new cases in the voting rights field during its first 20 months, compared to nearly a dozen in the first 12 months of the Carter administration.

Sometimes, hearing that term 'the exclusionary rule'—this is a rule—it isn't a law; it's case law. It was a judicial decision once made that now has evidence thrown out of court even if they feel there was some technical violation in the way that the evidence was obtained. . . . (11/17/82)

Wriggle, wriggle. Reagan may not be crazy about the exclusionary rule, but that's no reason to pretend it's not law. The rule, which prohibits the use of evidence obtained in violation of the US Constitution, has been read by the Supreme Court from the 4th, 5th, and 6th amendments.

The big spenders . . . even drove prayer out of the classrooms. (TV commercial, 10/31/82)

School prayer was abolished in 1962 by the Supreme Court's ruling in *Engle* v. *Vitale*. The Court does spend money on its operations, but it uses funds appropriated by Congress. When asked by the *New York Times* to identify the "big spenders," Mort Allin, an assistant White House press secretary, could not be specific. "They know who they are," he said.

NEWS ITEM

Upon signing an Executive Order reversing a 30-year trend toward less government secrecy, Reagan asserted that it would enhance "protection for national security information without permitting excessive classification of documents." Yet at a briefing for reporters following the signing, government officials acknowledged that *not one new provision* of the Order could be said to have been aimed at preventing overclassification or encouraging declassification of government records. (*Wash. Post,* 4/3/82)

SPECIAL REPORT #6

Tax-Exempt Status

On January 8, 1982, the Reagan administration announced that it wanted to repeal a 12-year-old policy denying tax exemptions to private schools that discriminate on the basis of race. Critics howled. The *New York Times,* for example, asserted that the "Reagan administration is picking the pocket of every American taxpayer to subsidize racism in education." (1/19/82) As the story mushroomed, President Reagan used several rather large brushstrokes to paint himself into a corner as he attempted to explain why his administration did what it did.

1/12/82:

" *I am . . . opposed to administrative agencies exercising powers that the Constitution assigns to the Congress. Such agencies, no matter how well intentioned, cannot be allowed to govern by administrative fiat. That was the sole basis of the decision announced by the Treasury Department last Friday.* **"**

The IRS was never acting by "administrative fiat." The Supreme Court in *Coit* v. *Green* (1971) explicitly concluded that the IRS *did* have a legal basis for its policy. And that policy was certainly not the IRS's own idea. When the case challenging the tax-exempt status of these schools came before the courts, the IRS fought it, maintaining that there was no constitutional obligation to use the tax laws to pursue school desegregation.

1/19/82:

" *What we were trying to correct was a procedure that we thought had no basis in law, that the IRS had actually formed a social law and was enforcing that social law. And we think that that's a bad precedent and is a bad thing to do, and so, there was no basis in the law for what they were doing.* **"**

" *I didn't know there were any [segregated schools]. Maybe I should have, but I didn't. I was under the impression that the problem of segregated schools had been settled.* **"** (Wash. Post, 5/12/82)

The law in the matter had been made clear by two Courts of Appeal and affirmed by the Supreme Court. For the past 12 years, the law has forbidden the IRS from giving tax-exempt "charity" status to discriminatory schools.

1/20/82:

❝ *I didn't know at the time [of the Executive Order] that there was a legal case pending.* ❞

Or so the President told William Raspberry of the *Washington Post.* The legal case Reagan was referring to was *Bob Jones University* v. *the United States,* which focused on the very issue of tax exempt status for segregated schools. However, according to a copy of a White House memo obtained by CBS News, the President *did* know of the case. The memo states that House Republican Whip Trent Lott (Miss.) "writes regarding pending cases concerning the tax exempt status of church schools. Indicates that the Supreme Court has now agreed to review case of *Bob Jones University* v. *the United States,* and urges you to intervene in that particular case." To the right of that summary, in the space reserved for comments, Reagan wrote: "I think we should."

1/21/82 (Wash. Post):

❝ *I'm the originator of the whole thing.* ❞

Fine.

THE REST OF HIM
Miscellaneous Distortions

Many of Ronald Reagan's distortions defy strict categorization. Over the years he has felt called upon to misstate the facts on a wide range of subjects. Sooner or later, it seems, he gets almost everything wrong. The result is a broad miscellany of error that proves an easily forgotten lesson: Ronald Reagan's grasp of detail is amazing. It's accuracy that gives him trouble.

FALSE ALARM ➤

66 *In this week of tragedy, six policemen in Chicago have been killed in the line of duty.* 99 (*L.A. Times*, 6/14/68)

Respect for law and order had not sunk that year to the depths Reagan imagined. Chicago police records showed that only two officers had died on duty *since January 1, 1968,* one on June 5, and the other on May 4. The week of tragedy never existed.

66 *[McGovern] did not become a peace advocate until . . . 1968 when he contracted Potomac fever. And he is still infected.* 99 (*L.A. Times*, 10/16/72)

McGovern first voiced opposition to Vietnam as a military boondoggle in 1963—that's five years before 1968. The day after he voted for the Tonkin Gulf resolution, he read into the congressional record his desire that no one construe his vote as support for growing involvement in Vietnam. On January 15, 1965—that's three years before 1968—he declared his opposition in a major speech. From that point on, he opposed every move to escalate bombing, increase troop strength, expand ground operations, etc.

NEWS ITEM

Governor Reagan's comment on the distribution of food in San Francisco demanded by Patty Hearst's kidnappers: "It's just too bad we can't have an epidemic of botulism." (*L.A. Times*, 3/7/74)

❝ To me, the simple argument is this: Is or is not the unborn child a human being? And from all that I learned in dealing with legislation on our state level, I am convinced that you are taking a human life when you interrupt a pregnancy. There's only one basis upon which we justify taking human life, and that's self-defense. ❞ (US News & World Report, 5/31/76)

The legislation on the state level to which Ronald Reagan is referring was one of the most liberal abortion bills in the country. He signed it into law in 1967. And, it should be pointed out, every year thereafter, he also signed, without a peep, expenditure legislation targeting federal funds to finance abortions. Anthony C. Beilenson, who, as a state legislator authored the original measure, believes the liberal abortion law was one of the factors in the reduced size of welfare families—a big plus in Governor Reagan's highly touted crusade to trim the state's welfare rolls.

❝ Somehow they [young people] never seem to have heard the other side. Never heard, for example, that marijuana contains 300 or more chemicals and 60 of those are found in no other plant. ❞ (Radio, Mar. 1979)

Before you get too excited, put this in perspective—tobacco smoke contains more than 3,000 chemicals.

❝ I had a great deal of sympathy [for blacklisted Hollywood actors], but I had just as much sympathy for the people whose careers were ruined by the Communists. They had a list, and if you were on their latest the phone stopped ringing and you didn't get called for parts anymore. They had more influence in the picture business than anyone has yet admitted. ❞ (Christian Science Monitor, 5/14/79)

This interesting account of the period of blacklisting in Holly-

Q: "Governor, do you think homosexuals should be barred from public office in the United States?"

A: "Certainly they should be barred from the Department of Beaches and Parks." (L.A. Times, 12/5/67)

◀ FALSE ALARM

WHAT A DIFFERENCE A DAY MAKES

2/18/80:

"How do you tell who the Polish fellow is at a cockfight? He's the one with the duck. How do you tell who the Italian is at the cockfight? He's the one who bets on the duck. How do you know the Mafia was there? The duck wins." (*Wash. Star*, 2/18/80)

2/19/80:

"I don't like that type of humor, and in a conversation about stories once, this came about with one of the reporters on the plane and I had given this as an example. And on the bus, he [the reporter] asked me the other day, he said, 'What was the sequence of that story,' and I paused and told him, and . . . I think it's a cheap shot to use it."
(*Wash. Post*, 2/19/80)

wood has never been corroborated. Countless books and articles have discussed the blacklisting *of* suspected Communists, but there seems to be woefully scarce examination of blacklisting *by* Communists. Frankly, it is hard to believe that the likes of Louis B. Mayer or Harry Cohn would have let lefties interfere in the operation of their studios, but you never can tell.

66 *Shouldn't we ask if anyone has done a comparison of the situation before there was such education in the schools and after? I've had a report from one district that the venereal disease rate among young people in that district went up 800% in the first few years after sex education became a part of the curriculum.* 99 (Radio, June 1979)

Since the school district is not named, it is difficult to track down the source of this report. However, a spokesman at the Atlanta Centers for Disease Control's VD division said they didn't know of any such circumstance and had not received such a report. He added that an 800% increase would be considered "a tremendous percentage rise in any communicable disease." Both Planned Parenthood of America and the Sex Information and Education Council said they "had never heard of such a thing." A spokeswoman at the American Social Health Association said that as far as she knew, no studies on a correlation between VD and sex ed had been done, and she had "no idea of what that figure is based on."

66 *As president, I would be younger than all the heads of state I would have to deal with except Margaret Thatcher.* 99 (*Wash. Star*, 11/12/79)

Reagan, who was 68 years old at the time, also made this assertion to Tom Brokaw on the "Today" show, who pointed out that Giscard d'Estaing of France would be younger. "Who?" responded Reagan. "Yes, possibly, not an awful lot more." Giscard d'Estaing was, at the time, 53. Chancellor Schmidt and Anwar Sadat were 60. Menachim Begin was 66. Lopez Portillo of Mexico was 59. Joe Clark of Canada, 40. And so on.

HUH???

Q: "Governor, do you consider yourself born again?"

A: "Well, I know what many of those who use that term mean by it. But in my own situation it was not in the religion, or the church that I was raised in, the Christian Church. But there you were baptized when you yourself decided that you were, as the Bible says, as the Bible puts it, that that is being born again. Within the context of the Bible, yes, by being baptized." (New York Times, 5/27/80)

I have been told that some of the Iranians coming to this country are here to create disturbances and to form terrorist groups, and immigration officials know this because some of the things they found in their luggage, yet the State Department has said to the immigration people, 'Don't rock the boat.' (Time, 4/1/80)

Reporters asked Reagan for corroborating evidence for this rather serious allegation—neither he nor his staff was able to provide any. It was not brought up again.

I am glad to be here where you're feeling it firsthand with the economic problems that have been committed, and he's [Carter's] opening his campaign down in the city that gave birth to and is the parent body of the Ku Klux Klan. (New York Times, 9/2/80)

Aside from the question of taste in kicking off his drive for the presidency with a reference to the Klan, the facts are skewed. Carter was in Tuscumbia, Alabama. The Klan is traditionally thought to have been founded in 1866 in Pulaski, Tennessee.

◄ LITTLE KNOWN FUN FACT

President Carter has yet to be in one [debate], going clear back to when he ran for governor of Georgia and he reneged on a commitment to debate his opponent there. (10/13/80)

Jimmy Carter debated President Gerald Ford three times in

the 1976 presidential campaign; the audiences averaged 60 million.

All we're doing is what every administration before us has done and we hadn't been doing. (1/19/82)

Reagan made this statement in response to a question about a recently issued presidential directive that required administration officials to clear interviews with the press. According to Patricia Bario, deputy press secretary to President Carter, the Carter administration required "no preclearance at all." The Carter White House requested that officials notify it only after accepting a spot on a Sunday or morning TV show.

I think we're ahead of just about anyone at this point with regard to the appointment of women to high positions in our government. (6/30/82)

Not ahead, not at that point. In the first 16 months of Carter's administration, he appointed 65 women out of 637 appointees to positions requiring Senate confirmation—or 10.2%. Under President Reagan, of the 679 people appointed to administrative positions requiring Senate confirmation, 51 were women—7.5%. And Sandra Day O'Connor notwithstanding, as of May 1982, the President had appointed only four women to 66 judicial positions—6%. By the end of his term, Carter had appointed women to 42 of 260 judicial openings—15.8%. A year after the President's statement, the US Civil Rights Commission said that it was "disappointed and concerned" about Reagan's record of appointing women and minorities to his administration, the federal judiciary, the US Attorney's Office, and the foreign service.

David Stockman was betrayed by a longtime friend who

distorted and misinterpreted things that had been said in complete confidence and the understanding that it was off the record. . . . **" ** (*People*, 12/27/82)

David Stockman has never alleged that William Grieder, author of the December 1981 article in *The Atlantic* magazine called "The Education of David Stockman," violated his confidence. Grieder based his article on taped, on-the-record conversations with Stockman, who proved quite capable of betraying himself.

" *It probably wasn't too much different from the press rushing into print with the Pentagon Papers, which were stolen—they were classified and it was against the law.* **"** (6/28/83)

"It" is completely different. This attempt by Reagan to wriggle out of the ethical problems raised by the alleged filching of Carter debate documents—"Debategate"—misfires. In *The New York Times Co.* v. *United States,* the Supreme Court ruled 6–3 that it was *not* "against the law" for the press to publish the Pentagon Papers. Nor has any court ever concluded the papers were "stolen." The criminal case against Daniel Ellsberg was thrown out of court. And in any event, it's hard to see how he could have stolen them since they were lawfully in his Pentagon office before publication.

NEWS ITEM

In April 1981, President Reagan pardoned two former FBI officials convicted of conspiracy for authorizing illegal break-ins of homes. "The record demonstrates that they acted not with criminal intent," he said, "but in the belief that they had grants of authority reaching to the highest levels of government." (*Newsweek,* 4/27/81) That's the exact opposite of the truth, for the jury specifically found that the two defendants *had* acted without the approval of higher-ups and in the full knowledge that such break-ins were unlawful. "We tried exactly that issue before the jury for eight weeks," said prosecuter John W. Nields, Jr.

TALL TALE ➡

In an interview aboard Air Force One, Reagan explained that offshore oil drilling near Santa Barbara, California, was not just a money-making operation but was critical to averting an undersea oil spill in the event of an earthquake. Because the oil was near an active fault, he went on, it was imperative to "drill, get it out, and remove that permanent threat that lies off the coast." (2/17/85) **The permanent threat is, however, not very great: according to the Minerals Management Service of the Department of the Interior, there is no known instance of an earthquake causing a large-scale leakage of oil through the ocean floor.**

❝*I'm delighted in telling about the town that decided in the interest of safety, they were going to raise all their street signs and everything that were only five feet high to seven feet high. And the Federal government came along and said, 'We've got a program that'll do that for you.' Well, it was quite an undertaking to change the height of all these. The Federal government's idea was they'd lower the streets two feet.* ❞ (2/9/82)

Boston Globe reporter Curtis Wilkie asked the White House to provide supporting evidence. As of July 1987, it hadn't.

❝*I think the fact that children have been born even down to the three-month stage and have lived, the record shows, to become normal human beings . . .* ❞ (*Wash. Post*, 8/2/83)

Dr. Douglas Richardson, attending physician at the neonatal Intensive Care Unit of Harvard Medical School's Brigham and Women's Hospital, says that survival of a three-month fetus would be "physiologically impossible." Even survival of an infant born at 23½ weeks (nearly 6 months) is "exceedingly rare . . . almost unprecedented."

❝*We are committed to appointing outstanding blacks, Hispanics, and women to judicial and top-level policy-making positions in our administration. . . . In our first two years we appointed more women to top posts than any administration before us.* ❞ (8/1/83)

According to the US Civil Rights Commission, here's how Reagan fared in the three categories he cited: blacks and Hispanics appointed to the federal judiciary under Carter, 22.1%, under Reagan, 3.3%; women appointed to the federal judiciary under Carter, 15.1%, under Reagan, 8.3%; women appointed to all posts under Carter, 22%, under Reagan, 8%.

FALSE ALARM

"In the 1982 election, it was made apparent that some of those [feminists] who are most active in this are most active if it's in behalf of the Democratic candidates. Let me just point out, we had some fine Republican women candidates, and they didn't get any help or support . . ." (U.S.A. Today, 8/27/83)

The California GOP Senate primary candidate in 1982, one Maureen Elizabeth Reagan, received the support of the National Women's Political Caucus.

TALL TALE

"The young ball-turret gunner was wounded, and they couldn't get him out of the [B-17] turret there while flying. . . . The last man to leave saw the commander sit down on the floor. He took the boy's hand and said, 'Never mind, son, we'll ride it down together.' Congressional Medal of Honor, posthumously awarded." (12/12/83)

Pulitzer Prize for Fiction, immediately awarded. Lars-Erik Nelson of the *New York Daily News* reviewed the citations for all 434 Medals of Honor awarded in World War II and could not find this story. He did, however, discover two other possible sources for this account of heroism: the 1944 Dana Andrews movie, *Wing and a Prayer,* or a 1944 story from the *New York Herald Tribune* that recounted a tale told by an Air Force public relations officer "which has become a legend."

"You asked about the case I mentioned of a child not being allowed to say grace in the school cafeteria. Without looking it up, I believe that the locale was New York and that it was children, not child. The school authorities thought they were required to forbid the practice. Evidently some parents made a case of it, and the courts upheld the school authorities." (Letter to Norman Lear, 6/25/84)

In 1963, the Second Circuit Court of Appeals in *Stein* v. *Oshinsky* prohibited *recited prayers* in classrooms by groups of children, *not* individual prayer by a child in a school cafeteria. Each of those children remained free to pray individually before, during, and after classes, and most assuredly in the school cafeteria. There is no law or court decision such as Reagan had described that prevents any student from praying whenever or wherever he or she wishes.

UNFAMILIAR QUOTATION ➤

❝ *One last thought, shouldn't someone tag Mr. Kennedy's bold new imaginative program with its proper age? Under the tousled boyish haircut it is still old Karl Marx—first launched a century ago. There is nothing new in the idea of a Govt. being Big Brother to us all. Hitler called his 'State Socialism' and way before him it was 'benevolent monarchy.'* **❞** (Letter to Richard Nixon, 1960)

When confronted with the text of his letter during the 1984 presidential campaign, Reagan denied he compared Hitler's program of national socialism with JFK's New Frontier: "I just said that if we start down the road to statism it leads to socialism. No matter how well it is presented, whether it goes to the left or to the right, it eventually winds up as totalitarianism."

❝ *Well, I don't think I've ever used the Bible to further political ends . . .* **❞** *(Wash. Post, 2/22/85)*

Wrong. Here's what he told the National Religious Broadcasters just two weeks before: "We mean to maintain a strong defense, because only with a strong defense can we preserve the peace we cherish. And I found myself wanting to remind you of what Jesus said in Luke 14:31: 'Oh, what king, when he sets out to . . . meet another king in battle will not first sit down and take counsel whether he is strong enough with 10,000 men to encounter the one coming against him with 20,000.' "

I've never believed in government funding of campaigns. The government decides who gets it. (Quoted in James J. Kilpatrick's syndicated column, 6/10/85)

All presidential candidates qualify for matching funds if they raise $5,000 in each of 20 states with no single contributor giving more than $250, regardless of the candidate's party, position, and ideology; and then major party candidates receive full public funding in their general elections. For someone whose 1980 and 1984 presidential campaigns received over $70 million in federal matching funds, the president doth protest too much.

Now, we all know we're up against an opponent [Tim Wirth] who has a habit of outspending his rivals in a big way, and this campaign is no exception. (9/8/86)

Reagan is exaggerating "in a big way." According to data from the Federal Elections Commission, Democrat Tim Wirth spent $3,787,202 on the 1986 Senate race in Colorado, a mere $1,625 more than what his Republican opponent, Ken Kramer, spent. However, these campaign totals do not include independent expenditures from other organizations. Over $819,000 was spent on Kramer's behalf, while Wirth was the indirect beneficiary of some $7,478 in outside expenditures.

FALSE ALARM

MISSION IMPOSSIBLE
Contra-dictions on Contragate

As the Arms-for-the-Ayatollah/Cash-for-the-Contras scandal unfolded in Washington, Beirut, Jerusalem, Teheran, Geneva, Miami, and Managua, the White House maintained the unimpeachable defense of presidential ignorance. The official party line was that Reagan was busy doodling cowboys and horses while NSC aide Lt. Col. Oliver ("Blood and Guts") North was doodling elaborate flow charts of lawyers, guns, and money. When a C-123K transport plane involved in the contra supply operations crashed in Nicaragua in early October of 1986 and a lone survivor was taken prisoner, Reagan's weather vane of truth pointed to "no Government connection with it at all." Seven months later, in the face of congressional testimony that he had a much more active role, the weather vane swung around, and suddenly private aid "was my idea to begin with." *About face, march!*

PROBLEM SOLVING

"*Surround yourself with the best people you can find, delegate authority, and don't interfere.***"** (*Fortune,* Sept. 1986)

"*Since US government contact began with Iran, there's been no evidence of Iranian Government complicity in acts of terrorism against the United States.***"** (11/13/86)

Yet as Reagan admitted six days later, Iran *was* kept on the US government list of states which sponsor terrorism. In fact, since September 9 of that year (long after the first US government contacts began), three more Americans were taken hostage by Iranian-backed factions in Lebanon.

"*Geography explains why the Soviet Union has sent an army into Afghanistan . . . and, if they could, Iran. . . . America's longstanding goals in the region have been to help preserve Iran's independence from Soviet domination.***"** (11/13/86)

On March 19, 1987, CIA officials Richard J. Kerr and Graham Fuller told the *New York Times* they had advised the White

House in 1985 that "there was no imminent threat that the Soviet Union would gain significant influence in Iran."

Q: "Mr. President, was there any U.S. involvement in this flight over Nicaragua—carrying the arms—any involvement whatsoever?"

RR: *"I'm glad you asked. Absolutely not. . . . While they're American citizens, there is no government connection with that at all."* (10/8/86)

Wrong. The October 5, 1986, downing of a C-123K cargo plane by Sandinista forces, and the capture of a survivor, Eugene Hasenfus, marked the end of a widespread network of private and covert US government aid to the Nicaraguan rebels. Congressional testimony disclosed that the following government officials actively supported or had prior knowledge of the network and/or the Hasenfus flight:

1. Lieutenant Colonel Oliver North, National Security Council aide (kept national security advisers Robert McFarlane and Vice-Admiral John Poindexter apprised of the contra resupply efforts).
2. Donald Gregg, national security adviser to Vice-President George Bush (briefed by a former CIA agent on contra resupply activities out of the Ilopango Air Base in El Salvador—headquarters of that country's air force.
3. Army Colonel James Steele, head of the U.S. military mission in El Salvador (closely monitored the contra resupply missions out of El Salvador; paid the Salvadoran military for fuel for use by the flights).

On October 12, 1986, North sent a computer message to former national security adviser Robert McFarlane: "We urgently need to find a high-powered lawyer and benefactor who can raise a legal defense fund for Hasenfus."

130

At first the President seemed to indicate to the Tower Commission investigating the Irangate scandal that sometime in August 1985 "he approved the shipment of arms by Israel to Iran." Reagan's memory shifted and he stated to the Commission that "he had been 'surprised' that the Israelis had shipped arms to Iran," and concluded he must not have approved the transfer. Next, the President decided he had remembered wrong in both instances. In fact he had no memory of the transaction. "I let myself be influenced by others' recollections, not my own," he wrote in a letter to the Commission (2/2/87). "Try as I might, I cannot recall anything whatsoever about whether I approved replenishment of Israeli stocks around August of 1985. My answer therefore and the simple truth is, I don't remember —period."

Reversing Ground I

❝*We did not—repeat, did not—trade weapons or anything else for hostages, nor will we.* ❞ (11/13/86)

❝*To eliminate the widespread but mistaken perception that we have been exchanging arms for hostages, I have directed that no further sales of arms of any kind be sent to Iran.* ❞ (11/19/86)

❝*Let me just say it was not my intent to do business with Khomeini, to trade weapons for hostages, nor to undercut our policy of anti-terrorism.* ❞ (12/6/86)

❝*A few months ago I told the American people I did not trade arms for hostages. My heart and my best intentions still tell me that's true, but the facts and the evidence tell me it is not.* ❞ (3/4/87)

❝*It sort of settled down to just trading arms for hostages, and that's a little like paying ransom to a kidnapper.* ❞ (3/26/87)

Well, was it a straight "arms-for-hostages" deal? Yes, said former National Security Council director John Poindexter. He told the Iran-Contra hearings that on December 5, 1985, the President signed an intelligence finding that "gave that same impression." It was retroactive authorization for a November 1985 Israeli deal to sell Hawk antiaircraft missiles to Iran strictly as an attempt to free American hostages held in Lebanon.

Reversing Ground II

"With regard to whether private individuals were giving money to support the contras, yes, I was aware that there were people doing that. But there was nothing in the nature of a solicitation by my administration, to my knowledge, of anyone to do with that. (5/3/87)

"I don't know how that money [private aid to the contras] was to be used and I have no knowledge that there was ever any solicitation by our people with these people. (5/5/87)

"There was no solicitation that I know of or anything of the kind. I did know, and had been informed, that he [King Fahd of Saudi Arabia] was helping, but I never brought it up. (5/13/87)

"As a matter of fact, I was very definitely involved in the decisions about [private] support to the freedom fighters. It was my idea to begin with. (5/15/87)

"I don't know who they [private contributors] were, and I never asked, and I never asked how they did it. (5/27/87)

"It was not a mistake."
(11/19/86)

"I didn't make a mistake."
(11/24/86)

"I do not think it was a mistake." (11/26/86)

"Mistakes were made."
(12/6/86)

". . . serious mistakes were made." (1/27/87)

"It was a mistake."
(3/4/87)

Q: "At your last news conference, four months ago, you said that Israel had nothing—the US had nothing to do with Israeli arms shipments to Iran when you knew that that was not true. Why did you say that?"

A: "... It was evidently just a misstatement on my part. I did not know that I had said it in such a way as to seemingly deny Israel's participation. And when they told me this, and when I finished bumping my head, I said to them, 'Quick! Write down a correction of this.' ... We've got to get this message to all of you before you went to work on your stories." (3/19/87)

The misstatement was repeated four times during the news conference and it was White House chief of staff Donald Regan, not Reagan, who realized that it was a mistake and had the correction issued.

❝This [the TOW anti-tank missile] is a purely defensive weapon. It is a shoulder-carried weapon. And we don't think that in this defensive thing—we didn't add to any offensive power on the part of Iran.❞ (11/19/86)

Was the President thinking of Paul Bunyan's shoulders? The "basic" TOW missile is nearly four feet long, and weighs 56.3 lbs. The US Marine Corps says the missile can be fired from a tripod, or, using a special mount, from a quarter-ton truck, jeep, or helicopter. The complete system requires a 4-man crew. While anti-tank missiles are generally defensive in nature, during an *offensive* maneuver Iran could use mobile TOWs to destroy Iraqi tanks before they attack.

❝We did not condone and do not condone the shipment of arms from other countries.❞ (11/19/86)

Minutes after the end of the President's November 19 press conference, his first on the subject of the Iran arms scandal, the White House issued a statement which said, in part, "There was a third country involved in our secret project with Iran."

❝The mission was served that made us waive temporarily [the arms embargo] for that really miniscule amount of spare parts and defensive weapons ... everything that we sold them could be put in one cargo plane, and there would be plenty of room left over.❞ (11/19/86)

Miniscule? Plenty of room left over? Hardly. In all, the US sold Iran or authorized Israel to sell Iran 2,008 TOW anti-tank missiles and at least twelve pallets of HAWK anti-aircraft missile parts. Additionally, 120 HAWK anti-aircraft missiles were to be sent in an abortive deal in November 1985. A single TOW missile weighs 56.3 lbs. A single HAWK missile weighs 1,400 lbs. and its launcher weighs 4,326 lbs. The Air Force's C-5B cargo plane, the largest-capacity cargo plane used by the US military, can transport a maximum of 242,500 lbs. The missiles authorized for shipment (2,008 TOWs and 120 HAWKS) weighed *281,050 lbs.* In fact, multiple flights of normal cargo jets were used to transport all the missiles and gear sold to Iran.

◄ **WISHFUL THINKING DEPT.**

❝*After my speech [on 11/13/86], some 84% of those people who called in supported me. It was the biggest outpouring of calls they've ever had.***❞** (11/26/86)

White House spokesman Larry Speakes put the total at 1,559 telephone calls, with another 2,666 calls logged in the following week, after the President's news conference. The all-time 24-hour record for calls after a presidential address is 200,000, following President Nixon's resignation speech.

◄ **DEPT. OF RETRACTIONS**

❝*[It was an] effort to establish a relationship with responsible moderates in Iran.***❞** (12/6/86)

That's not what Vice-President George Bush heard on July 29, 1986. Bush was told by Amiram Nir, an Israeli intermediary, that "we are dealing with the most radical elements. . . . They can deliver . . . that's for sure."

❝*What is driving me up the wall is that this wasn't a failure until the press got a tip from that rag in Beirut and began to play it up.***❞** (11/26/86)

That's not how the Tower Commission saw it. The process, they concluded, was fundamentally flawed because the trading of arms for hostages was implicit from the beginning. As former Secretary of State Edmund Muskie, a member of the Tower board put it, "The policy was a wrong policy, and it was the President's policy."

NEWS ITEM
"Don't talk TOWS, don't talk specifics." (President Reagan to top aides at a private White House meeting about how to stem the breaking Iran-Contra stories, 11/10/86)

> *There is nothing in [the Boland Amendment] that prevents citizens—individuals or groups—from offering aid of whatever kind they wanted to. And my interpretation was that it was not restrictive on the national security adviser or National Security Council. . . . And there is nothing that has ever been in the Boland Amendment that could keep me from asking other people to help [the rebels].* U.S. News & World Report, 5/25/87)

Rather than ask other people to help fund the contras, Reagan should have asked other people to help interpret the Boland Amendment. For here the President was relying on the legal interpretation of President's Intelligence Oversight Board general counsel Bretton G. Sciaroni, who had twice failed the California bar exam, twice failed the District of Columbia bar exam, and who took the Pennsylvania bar exam in the hope of passing and obtaining automatic waiver into the District of Columbia bar. Sciaroni revealed in congressional testimony he had spent a grand total of thirty-five minutes (five minutes with NSC aide Lieutenant Colonel Oliver North, and half an hour with NSC counsel Commander Paul Thompson) in August 1985 investigating whether the NSC was covered by the Boland Amendment. In his *first* legislative opinion, Sciaroni held that aid to the contras by the NSC was *not* prohibited by the Boland Amendment because the NSC was not "involved in intelligence activities." In an October 10, 1984, House floor statement, however, Rep. Edward Boland (D-Mass.) had explained that his amendment barred *all* U.S. support for the contras, with "no exceptions."

> *I told you all the truth that first day after . . . everything hit the fan.* (6/11/87)

Uh-huh.

A VERY FOREIGN POLICY

They are all different countries out there, and Ronald Reagan has ideas about every one of them. Nicaragua is up against virtuous freedom fighters who never supported the right-wing dictator Anastasio Somoza. Germany is populated entirely by baby-boomers who had nothing to do with the Holocaust. Nuclear proliferation is not a problem, since small countries show only slight interest in having nuclear weapons of their own. Erroneous information like that works fine for Reagan as long as he doesn't actually use it to make policy. Unfortunately, he's making policy all the time. So when reality—and occasionally Congress—intrudes on this delicate process, the President has to produce further "insights" to bolster his position. It's a never-ending, time-consuming business, but Reagan has always managed to come up with aides—like John Poindexter, Bud McFarlane, and Elliott Abrams—to see him through.

❝*I think we're pretty well on our way to, if not entirely eliminating nuclear proliferation, holding it down to where a country might have a weapon or two, but they're not going to have enough to threaten the world.*❞ (1/22/83)

► **WISHFUL THINKING DEPT.**

At least four nations have gained or enhanced their nuclear capability since Reagan came to office: India, which exploded one nuclear bomb in 1974, increased plutonium production by over 1,000% over the last thirteen years; Israel, which reportedly built 30 to 60 nuclear weapons during Reagan's term in office and has successfully deployed its own nuclear-capable Jericho II missiles; Pakistan, which is believed to have produced one or two atomic weapons in 1986; and South Africa, which produced and began stockpiling weapons-grade material in 1981, and which may have 12 to 15 atomic devices.

❝*The results of this self-proclaimed unity between the Sandinistas and the terrorists in the PLO are evident for all the*

► **FALSE ALARM**

world to see and an evil echo of history. Virtually the entire Jewish community in Nicaragua has been frightened into exile . . . " (7/20/83)

Not according to members of his own administration. Four days before Reagan made this statement, US ambassador to Nicaragua Anthony Quainton sent a confidential cable to Secretary of State George Shultz, which concluded that the Jewish community of Nicaragua were not victims of anti-Semitism, but had been treated the same as "other Nicaraguans of the middle and upper classes who have been persecuted because of their political or financial positions."

FALSE ALARM ➤

"[Grenadian leader Maurice Bishop] sought the help of Cuba in building an airport, which he claimed was for tourist trade, but which looked suspiciously suitable for military aircraft, including Soviet-built long-range bombers. " (10/27/83)

And the volleyball courts at Club Med looked suspiciously like grenade arsenals. Bishop's airport at Port Salines was financed, in part, by the British government and the European Common Market, and a British firm was the prime contractor. Contrary to military specifications, the Port Salines facility had no protected fuel dumps or hardened bays for parked warplanes. In fact, the 9,000-foot runway is consistent with other Caribbean airstrips (San Juan—10,000 feet: Barbados—9,000 feet) necessary for takeoffs by fully loaded charter flights.

"We had to assume that several hundred Cubans working on the [Grenada] airport could be military reserves. Well, as it turned out, the number was much larger, and they were a military force. Six hundred of them have been taken prisoner. " (10/27/83)

One week later, on November 2, US military authorities in Grenada had reclassified most of the Cuban prisoners as workers, with only about 100 "combatants."

"Two hours ago we released the first photos from Grenada. They included pictures of a warehouse of military equipment—one of three we've uncovered so far. This warehouse contained weapons and ammunition stacked almost to the ceiling, enough to supply thousands of terrorists.**"** (10/27/83)

Out of six warehouses located by US officials, three contained no weapons. The principal arms storage shed was about one-quarter full and included approximately 190 crates of assorted small arms. Some were modern Soviet-made weapons, but more were from WWII and earlier; and one crate contained Marlin .30-caliber carbines manufactured in the 1870s.

"Winston Churchill . . . once said that Americans did not cross the ocean, cross the mountains, and cross the prairies because we're made of sugar candy.**"** (1/27/84)

Cross out "Americans" and substitute "Canadians." Churchill's tribute was addressed to the House of Commons in Ottawa.

"There is a small, violent right wing [in El Salvador] as opposed to democracy as are the guerrillas, but they are not part of the government.**"** (5/6/84)

Oh, but they *are* part of the government. Vice-President Bush a few months earlier met with 31 top military leaders and warned them that further American aid would not be forthcoming unless the death squads were curbed. As a result, death-squad murders dramatically declined.

"They [the Waffen SS and German Army soldiers buried at the Bitburg cemetery] were victims, just as surely as the victims in the concentration camps.**"** (4/18/85)

◄ UNFAMILIAR QUOTATION

After it was disclosed that a CIA manual advocated that the contras "neutralize" local Sandinista officials and "shoot" informers, Reagan dismissed the story as "a great big scare [because] there was nothing in that manual that had anything to do with assassinations or anything of that kind." When asked how a Nicaraguan official can be removed from office without violence, Reagan answered, "You just say to the fellow that's sitting there in the office, 'You're not in the office anymore.'" (11/3/84)

❝The program [aid to El Salvador] is a balanced combination of support for democracy, economic development, diplomacy, and security measures, with 70% of the dollars to be used for economic and social development.❞ (5/9/84)

Try 15%. A February 1985 report released by Sen. Mark Hatfield (R-Oreg.) and Reps. Jim Leach (R-Iowa) and George Miller (D-Cal.), concluded that direct and indirect military aid accounted for 75% of American assistance to El Salvador, while only 15% went toward economic development. The report criticized the administration's "insufficient, misleading, and, in some cases, false information to Congress."

❝No, I never defended Somoza.❞ (10/21/84)

Not never. In a January 2, 1978, broadcast made over California radio station KGO, Reagan insisted that "[Somoza's Nicaragua] has never been known as a major violator of human rights. Keep that in mind, for in recent months it has been getting a bad press." He added that Somoza had made progress against illiteracy, and praised his nation as a "staunch supporter of the United States in world forums, and . . . strongly anticommunist." (*The Nation,* 11/10/84)

❝Very few [of the German people are] alive that remember even the war, and certainly none of them who were adults and participating in any way.❞ (*Time,* 4/29/85)

Tell that to Klaus Barbie, a Gestapo chief in Nazi-occupied France, who, at the age of 73, was recently convicted of crimes against humanity. West German president Richard von Weizsäcker, 67 years old, and Franz Josef Strauss, the 73-year-old prime minister of Bavaria, are both veterans of Hitler's army, as are several hundreds of thousands of other German citizens.

❝_I received what seemed to be a private invitation to go to one of the concentration camps, and I didn't see any way that I, as a guest of the state and of the government of Germany, could take off on my own and go. . . ._**❞** (4/29/85)

The private invitation was, in fact, a letter from West German chancellor Helmut Kohl recommending that the President visit Dachau, while still maintaining his plans to visit the Bitburg cemetery. As one American official told Bernard Weinraub of the _New York Times,_ "The President was not hot to go to a camp. You know, he is a cheerful politician. He does not like to grovel in a grisly scene like Dachau. He was reluctant to go. I am not saying opposed, but there was a coolness. And nobody pushed him on it."

❝. . . _this cemetery—we only found out later, someone dug up the fact that there are about 30 graves of SS troops. These were the villains, as we know, that conducted the persecutions and all. But there are 2,000 [other German Army] graves there._**❞** (4/18/85)

The fact had to be literally "dug up." When presidential advance man Michael Deaver first scouted the cemetery for Reagan's wreath-laying, the ground was covered with snow and no one thought to ask about who was buried in Bitburg. When the snows melted, it was abundantly clear that 47 Waffen SS had graves in the cemetery. While not every German soldier endorsed Nazi genocide, history doesn't exactly exonerate the German Army. As Daniel Goldhagen wrote in _The New Republic_ (5/13/85), "In Serbia, which is today part of Yugoslavia, the army decided, on its own initiative, to exterminate the local Jewish population. Without the aid of the SS, the army shot 4,000 to 5,000 Jewish men, and condemned 15,000 women and children to concentration camps."

When asked about the security problems facing American embassies in light of the bombing of the Marine barracks in Lebanon, Reagan attributed the problem to the "near destruction of our intelligence capability in recent years—before we came here, the effort that somehow to say, well, spying is somehow dishonest and let's get rid of our intelligence agents—and we did that to a large extent." (9/26/84)

Reagan's implication that Jimmy Carter was somehow responsible for the upsurge in Middle East terrorism provoked such a furor that he felt compelled to call up his predecessor two days later to explain his remarks. In fact, CIA director William Casey acknowledged that post-Vietnam cuts in the CIA's budgets were reversed during Carter's administration. (_Wash. Post,_ 10/1/84)

DEPT. OF RETRACTIONS

"I do not believe . . . that the local commanders on the ground [in Beirut during the bombing of the Marine barracks], men who have already suffered quite enough, should be punished for not fully comprehending the nature of today's terrorist threat. If there is to be blame, it properly rests here in this office and with this president. And I accept responsibility for the bad as well as the good." (12/27/83)

"Mr. Mondale should know that the President of the United States did not order the Marines into that barracks. That was a command decision made by the commanders on the spot and based with what they thought was best for the men there." (10/21/84)

❝One of the many who wrote me about this visit was a young woman who had recently been bat mitzvahed. She urged me to lay the wreath at Bitburg cemetery in honor of the future of Germany, and that is what we have done. ❞ (*New York Daily News,* 5/8/85)

Not exactly. Thirteen-year-old Beth Flom did *not* urge the President to visit the Bitburg cemetery. Her letter to Reagan read in part: "Although I understand your position, I cannot bring myself to agree with your solution." She added, however, that *if* he went to Bitburg, he should do so not to honor the soldiers of the German Army and the SS buried there, but "in honor of the future of Germany." Reagan later apologized for having distorted the letter.

❝And the leaders of the contras were leaders in that revolution [against Somoza] also. ❞ (5/10/85)

Leaders during the revolution, *sí.* But on the other side. In March 1986, the Congressional Arms Control and Foreign Policy Caucus identified 12 out of 13 members of the "high command" of the Nicaraguan Democratic Force (FDN), the principal contra group, as former officers in Somoza's National Guard.

❝I did not openly criticize [former president Jimmy Carter for the Iranian hostage situation]. As a matter of fact, in the closing days of the campaign . . . I didn't say any word or make any statement on the situation. ❞ (*New York Daily News,* 6/19/85)

As a matter of fact, he did. For example: "I believe that this administration's foreign policy helped create the entire situation. . . . And I think the fact that they've been held there that long is a humiliation and a disgrace to this country." (10/21/80)

❝*Well, I think that we're concerned about the violence that was evident there [in the Philippines] and the possibility of fraud, although it could have been that all of that was occurring on both sides.***❞** (2/11/86)

It could have been, but it wasn't. Most independent accounts of the Philippine election, including a report by US diplomat Philip Habib to President Reagan, confirmed large-scale fraud by supporters of President Ferdinand Marcos. Responding the next day to Reagan's remarks, Corazón Aquino said, "I would wonder at the motives of a friend of democracy who chose to conspire with Mr. Marcos to cheat the Philippine people of their liberation."

❝*I think it's significant that Bayardo Arce, one of Nicaragua's nine commandantes, was the first foreigner asked to address the recent Soviet Party Congress.***❞** (3/6/86)

The first foreigner to make an address to the 27th Soviet Party Congress was Fidel Castro of Cuba. Bayardo Arce did not get a chance to speak until five days later. He had been preceded by about two dozen other foreign speakers, including those from Portugal, France, West Germany, India, Italy, and the United States.

❝*Gathered in Nicaragua already are . . . all the elements of international terror—from the PLO to Italy's Red Brigades.***❞** (3/16/86)

Neither the White House press office nor the State Department could provide proof of Reagan's assertions. The PLO has no representative in Nicaragua, and the Italian government denies any knowledge of the presence of Red Brigade representatives in Nicaragua.

◀ **WISHFUL THINKING DEPT.**

NEWS ITEM

Time magazine reported in March 1986 President Reagan's damning evaluation of a Nicaraguan national hero: "The man whom [the Sandinistas] honor, Sandino, he said he was a Communist." Three months later the President had changed his mind. "The commandantes even betrayed the memory of the Nicaraguan rebel leader Sandino, whose legacy they falsely claim. For the real Sandino, because he was a genuine nationalist, was opposed to communism." (6/24/86)

◀ **FALSE ALARM**

DEPT. OF RETRACTIONS

When Jesse Jackson obtained the release of captured American flier Lt. Robert Goodman, the President was all praise. "Reverend Jackson's mission was a personal mission of mercy," he glowed, "and he has earned our gratitude and admiration." (1/4/84) But when Jesse Jackson was planning to fly to Moscow to free dissident Andrei Sakharov, the President didn't think it was such a good idea: "It is a case that there is a law, the Logan Act, with regard to unauthorized personnel, civilians, simply going to . . . other countries and, in effect, negotiate with foreign governments. Now, that is the law of the land." (7/4/84)

❝The Sandinistas have even involved themselves in the international drug trade. I know every American parent concerned about the drug problem will be outraged to learn that top Nicaraguan government officials are deeply involved in drug trafficking.**❞** (3/16/86)

The US Drug Enforcement Administration is particularly concerned about the drug problem, yet they rebutted these charges two days after Reagan made them. The DEA had no information implicating "the Minister of Interior or other Nicaraguan officials. . . ." Quite the contrary, *Newsweek,* the *Wall Street Journal, NBC Nightly News,* and the CBS News program *West 57th* all subsequently reported on the link between contra weapons suppliers and the Central American drug trade.

❝We weren't out, in the sense of getting one man [Libyan leader Muammar Qaddafi], that we were dropping tons of bombs trying to blow him up. I don't think any of us would have shed tears if that had happened, but we were out to damage and destroy those facilities that were making it possible for that particular state, under his guidance, to back and support terrorism.**❞** (5/6/86)

Seymour Hersh, writing in the *New York Times Magazine,* concluded, after interviews with more than seventy current and former officials, that the primary objective of the April 14, 1986, bombing of Tripoli was to kill Muammar Qaddafi and his family. "There's no question that they were looking for Qaddafi," one Air Force intelligence officer told Hersh. "They were going to kill him." According to an Air Force pilot involved in highly classified special operations, "The assassination was the big thing."

> **"** *I don't believe [aiding the contras] was counter to our law. . . . These people were voluntarily offering help, just as we have seen in the past. We had a thing called the Abraham Lincoln Brigade in Spain in the civil war there.* **"** (3/19/87)

Here's what Reagan thought of the Brigade on October 25, 1984: "Well, if you get into the moral issue of it, we were certainly tested with regard to that Spanish Civil War I mentioned, because I would say that the individuals that went there [the antifascist Abraham Lincoln Brigade] were, in the opinion of most Americans, fighting on the wrong side."

LITTLE KNOWN FUN FACT

Following a half-hour lecture by the Lebanese Foreign Minister on the intricate realities of his country's many political factions: **"** *You know, your nose looks just like Danny Thomas'.* **"** (*The Nation,* 2/18/84)

Johannesburg

Somewhere in Ronald Reagan's theme-park imagination there is a faraway country called South Africa, which once practiced apartheid but has now seen the error of its ways. Indeed, it's morning in Ronald Reagan's South Africa, as they begin to do away with segregation and embrace racial brotherhood and universal suffrage, just as the United States did several decades ago. Reagan looks at South Africa through the lens of an all-American success story—the civil rights movement—and draws appealing parallels. But inaccurate ones, nevertheless. For, try as he might, he can't bring himself to accept a basic truth: the South Africa of today more closely resembles the America of 1860 than 1960. Sadly, the more fervently Reagan clings to "constructive engagement" with the "reformist" government of P. W. Botha, the more he confirms his *dis*engagement from reality.

"*I think to put it that way, that they [black marchers in South Africa] were simply killed and that the violence was coming totally from the law-and-order side, ignores the fact that there was rioting going on on behalf of others there.* **"** (3/21/85)

The President ignores the fact that a judge appointed by the South African government concluded that the charge that 20 demonstrators killed in Uitenhage had been throwing rocks at police "was fabricated . . . to justify the shooting."

WISHFUL THINKING DEPT. ➤

"*[South Africa has] eliminated the segregation that we once had in our own country, the type of thing where hotels and restaurants and places of entertainment and so forth were segregated—that has all been eliminated.* **"** (8/24/85)

That type of thing, as the White House later admitted, has not "all been eliminated." The Group Areas Act, segregating the areas where blacks, whites, Indians, and mixed-race

South Africans can live, is still in effect. Restrooms, cemeteries, and most beaches are still segregated.

> **❝***Blacks can buy property in heretofore white areas, they can own businesses in some 40 white-dominated districts.***❞**
> (8/26/85)

Sure, but not in South Africa. There has been no modification or relaxation of the Group Areas Act, whose provisions divide South Africa into white, colored, Indian, and black zones. Under the Act, blacks are still barred from owning property in white areas. The government is considering but has not passed a law which would enable blacks to operate businesses in white areas. Even if that proposal became law, blacks could not own either the buildings housing the businesses or the land underneath them, nor could they enter the white areas without express government approval.

> **❝***You see, this wouldn't have been necessary if I had what a president should have, which is line-item veto.***❞** (9/9/85)

◄ WISHFUL THINKING DEPT.

What a president should really have is some idea of what he's talking about. This explanation for his preempting by executive order the South Africa sanctions bill doesn't hold up, since every line-item proposal pending in Congress refers only to appropriations bills, not laws or executive orders affecting foreign affairs.

> **❝***The infamous pass laws have ended . . .***❞** (7/22/86)

Not quite. No sooner had South African blacks thrown away their passbooks than the government ordered them to carry universal identity documents at all times. These papers function as internal passports; without them, no black is allowed entry into white areas. The edifice of "influx control" remains intact, pass laws or no pass laws.

❝*Citizenship, wrongly stripped away, has been restored to nearly six million blacks.* **❞** (7/22/86)

No. According to South African government estimates, the Restoration of South Africa Citizenship Bill of 1986 covers only 1.75 million of the 9 million blacks who lost their South African citizenship when the government granted "independence" to the ethnic "homelands" of Bophuthatswana, Venda, Transkei, and Ciskei.

❝*In South Africa you're talking about a country, yes, we disagree, and find repugnant some of the practices of their government but they're not seeking to impose their government on other countries.* **❞** (8/12/86)

Is South Africa's occupation of neighboring Namibia "repugnant"? In the face of condemnations from the UN Security Council and the International Court of Justice, South Africa has imposed direct control over neighboring Namibia, chiefly through its 100,000 troops garrisoned there since 1980.

❝*And the one group that is in support of [sanctions against South Africa] is a group that very definitely has been the most radical. . . .* **❞** (8/12/86)

One group? Supporters of sanctions range from leading clergymen such as Desmond Tutu (Anglican Archbishop of Cape Town), Reverend Dr. Allan Boesak (Moderator of the Dutch Reformed Church), and Reverend Dr. Beyers Naude (former Secretary General of the South African Council of Churches), to the Congress of South African Trade Unions (COSATU), South Africa's largest independent labor federation, representing over half a million workers, and the United Democratic Front, an umbrella organization encompassing 600 community groups and labor unions.

DEFENSE & RUSSIA
Arming for Bear

The evil empire has a new tsar, and he has been getting some good press lately. But while Mikhail Gorbachev proposes peace, the President keeps using his ability to misstate and misspeak to come across as the heavy. To support his positions, Reagan has shown off his fictitious knowledge of Russian, enthusiastically misquoted Lenin, and come up with some surprising new insights into the history of America's nuclear defenses. Despite Reagan's efforts, opinion in Western Europe tilts in favor of General Secretary Gorbachev, a smiling politician with a message of good will. Our guy smiles too, but that's about it. After the Reykjavik Summit, five Republican senators met with Reagan in the Oval Office and asked whether he had advocated total disarmament with Gorbachev. Reagan's answer, according to a participant? He couldn't remember.

"*Evidence abounds that we cannot simply assume that agreements negotiated with the Soviet Union will be fulfilled. . . . We negotiated a biological weapons convention, but deadly yellow rain and other toxic agents fall on Hmong villages and Afghan encampments.* **"** (9/26/83)

Yes, it is yellow and it falls from the sky. But in 1982, Thai, British, and Canadian scientists examined samples of the "yellow rain" under microscopes and found that they all consisted mostly of grains of pollen. Based on this evidence, Harvard biologist Matthew Meselson and Yale honeybee expert Thomas Seeley discarded the idea of Soviet use of tricothecene mycotoxin biological warfare agents, and concluded in 1983 that the "yellow rain" was actually a shower of bee feces.

"*I read where a man in Moscow had been awarded [the*

PROBLEM SOLVING

"*If you've got everybody building defense, then nobody's going to start a war.* **"** (10/19/83)

◄ TALL TALE

HUH???

According to Strobe Talbott, author of *Deadly Gambits*, when Deputy Director of the CIA Adm. Bobby Inman was tutoring the President on the basic aspects of Soviet nuclear strength, Reagan asked, "Isn't the SS-19 their biggest missile?"

"No," replied Inman. "That's the SS-18."

"So," said Reagan, "they've even switched the numbers on their missiles in order to confuse us!"

"No," Inman explained, "it's we who assign those numbers to their weapons systems in the sequence that we observe them, Mr. President."

Soviet Union's] highest honor, their Gold Medal. . . . He was the man who buried that ice axe mountaineers—mountain climbers—carry in the head of Leon Trotsky. **99** (12/12/83)

Lars-Erik Nelson of the *New York Daily News* contacted the CIA about this story. They told him they have no evidence that the assassin in question, Ramon Mercader, received the Soviet Union's highest honor, the Order of Lenin with Gold Star. Excluding the Olympics, there is no such award as the "Gold Medal."

66 *In the last few years before we came here there was a 21% reduction in defense spending.* **99** (2/22/84)

The *Wall Street Journal* pointed out that military expenditures during the Carter administration *increased* by 65% (not adjusted for inflation). In fact, the defense budget went up in real terms every year during Carter's term. Undaunted, the White House defended the President's claim as a "fair and honest statement."

66 *I think the people should understand that two-thirds of the defense budget pays for pay and salary, or pay and pension.* **99** (10/7/84)

More like two-*tenths*. According to the Office of Management and Budget, only 22.8% of the defense budget goes to military personnel, which included retirement pay. Fully one-half of total defense expenditures goes to research and development, procurement, military construction, and nuclear warhead programs.

66 *Let me go back and recall the press conference when those words were spoken. They were in answer to a direct question and they weren't my words.* **99** (10/16/84)

Confused? So was the President. *US News & World Report* had asked him why he expected the Soviets to negotiate with the US after he had denounced them as folks who "lie" and who ran "an evil empire." Regan denied saying those words. Yet at his first presidential news conference, Reagan said that the Soviets "reserve unto themselves the right to commit any crime, to lie, to cheat." And in Orlando, Florida, on March 8, 1983, Reagan referred to "the aggressive impulses of an evil empire. . . ."

❝*Remember, the SALT II is nothing but a limitation on how fast you increase weapons.* **❞** (1/9/85)

SALT II placed specific and absolute limits on missiles and bombers. If it had been ratified by the United States, the Soviet Union would have been required to scrap some 250 of its most powerful missiles.

❝*One of the violations of [the USSR] has been that they were taking nuclear submarines out of action, but they were cutting them down and rebuilding them as cruise-missile-carrying submarines.* **❞** (2/21/85)

Only three weeks earlier the White House had released the 1985 *President's Report on Soviet Noncompliance with Arms Control Agreements,* which said: "Finding: The U.S. Government judges that the Soviet Union's conversion of a dismantled SSBN into a submarine longer than the original and carrying modern, long-range cruise missiles is not a violation of its political commitment under the SALT I interim agreement."

❝*The 21 [MX missiles are] . . . the first modernization of our land-based missiles in almost the lifetime of the men and women who are handling these weapons.* **❞** (4/2/85)

FALSE ALARM

NEWS ITEM

During the '84 election debates, the President called attention to a Democratic campaign commercial about national defense, in which Mondale stands on the deck of an aircraft carrier. Reagan decided that it was the USS _Nimitz_ and said that if Mondale "had had his way when the _Nimitz_ was being planned, he would have been deep in the water out there because there wouldn't have been any _Nimitz_ to stand on." (10/21/84) Mondale aides pointed out that the ad was filmed aboard the USS _Midway_, which was commissioned in September 1945 —long before Mondale became a senator voting on military appropriations. (*UPI,* 10/22/84)

LITTLE KNOWN FUN FACT ➤

Then these weapons are being handled by preschoolers. The Defense Department completed several major improvements to land-based missiles throughout the 1970s and early 1980s, including: substituting newer and more reliable missiles and warheads; hardening silos; and upgrading launching and guidance systems. The latest component of the Minuteman III ICBM to be replaced was the MK-12A reentry vehicle in January 1983.

❝*As a matter of fact, as a percentage of the federal budget, we spent more on defense 15 years ago, and the world was a lot less dangerous.* ❞ (4/6/85)

In constant 1986 dollars, the Fiscal Year 1985 defense budget was $15 billion *higher* than in Fiscal Year 1970, even though the US was engaged in a land war in Southeast Asia in 1970. Yes, a larger portion of the earlier budget was spent on defense, but that's not surprising when you take into account the war, the proportionally lower levels of domestic spending, and a budget deficit of only $2.8 billion.

❝*Lenin made an eloquent statement. He said, 'We must take Eastern Europe. . . . We will organize the hordes of Asia. . . . We will move into Latin America. . . . We will not have to take the last bastion of capitalism, the United States. It will fall into our outstretched hands like overripe fruit.'* ❞ (9/9/85)

A chilling statement indeed, but unfortunately no one—not even the Library of Congress—has been able to find the source for it. Nor can the White House Press Office. Recently, someone did turn up a publication where this statement appeared—*The Blue Book of the John Birch Society,* written by Society founder Robert Welch in 1958.

❝*I'm no linguist, but I have been told that in the Russian language there isn't even a word for freedom.* 🎗🎗 (10/29/85)

The Russian word for "freedom" is *svoboda*. The Russian word for "gaffe" is *ogovorka*.

🎗🎗*We would not deploy [SDI] until we sit down with the other nations of the world and those that have nuclear arsenals and see if we cannot come to an agreement on which there will be deployment only if there is elimination of the nuclear weapons.* 🎗🎗 (11/4/85)

DEPT. OF RETRACTIONS

This stunning shift in the administration's position on deployment of a space-based missile defense system (suggesting we deploy a defensive system only when there are no *offensive* weapons around anymore) was dismissed the next day by White House spokesman Larry Speakes as "presidential imprecision."

🎗🎗*And we have fewer [warheads] than we had in 1969.* 🎗🎗 (11/4/85)

FALSE ALARM

No, we have more. According to the Center for Defense Information, the number of US strategic warheads rose from about 4,000 in 1970 to 11,492 by November 1985.

🎗🎗*And your research indicates the potential of [the recently cancelled Sergeant York mobile air-defense weapon], and you go forward. . . . And suddenly you find that something that looked good when you first planned it and ordered it has now been overtaken by a superior defense.* 🎗🎗 (12/4/85)

The Sergeant York weapon performed so poorly in its field tests that the real Sergeant Alvin York would have presented a greater threat to attacking Soviet aircraft with his World War I carbine. The Sergeant York was cancelled because it could not perform according to its original specifications. Its

"My fellow Americans, I am pleased to tell you today that I've signed legislation which outlaws Russia forever. The bombing begins in five minutes." (Testing his radio broadcast microphone, 8/11/84)

two 40mm anti-aircraft guns kept jamming, and its radar could not detect hovering helicopters, let alone incoming Soviet fighters—indeed, it functioned better as a homing device for Soviet radar-seeking missiles. By the time of its dishonorable discharge in August 1985, this gold-plated turkey had run up a bill of $1.8 billion.

❝*Now the biggest increases in defense spending are behind us. And that's why last summer I agreed to freeze defense funding for one year, and after that to resume a modest 3% annual growth [rate].*❞ (2/26/86)

Don't be so modest! Reagan's 1987 defense budget called for a hike of at least 12% over the 1986 amount, from $278.4 billion to $311.6 billion.

❝*[Gorbachev] is the first Russian leader to my knowledge that has ever voiced the idea of reducing and even eliminating nuclear weapons.*❞ (6/11/86)

Reagan's knowledge is, as usual, limited. The former US ambassador to Bulgaria, Raymond Garthoff, a member of the SALT I negotiating team and now a Sovietologist with the Brookings Institute, says, "Every Soviet leader from Stalin to Gorbachev has proposed eliminating nuclear weapons." For example, in 1946 the USSR turned down the Baruch plan (which favored the US) and proposed their own reduction plan (which favored *them* and was turned down by the US). Khrushchev offered general disarmament proposals in 1959 and 1962. Indeed, says Garthoff, "it wasn't until the early 1960s that the Soviets proposed any limitation other than banning nuclear weapons."

❝*We appointed the first Inspector General in the history of the Defense Department and virtually every case of fraud or* abuse has been uncovered by our Defense Department, our Inspector General. 99 (2/26/86)

Reagan's statement ignores some essential facts: his administration *opposed* legislation creating a Pentagon Inspector General, and sought to weaken its proposed authority every time Congress debated the issue. Alarmed by huge cost overruns, Congress sought an independent Inspector General for the Defense Department, but the White House wanted an Inspector General who would be under the control of the very people he was to investigate. Ultimately, Congress prevailed. Only after the Inspector General began uncovering examples of waste and contract abuse did Reagan begin celebrating the office's creation as an administration achievement.

66 *SDI, let me make it clear, is a non-nuclear defense.* 99 (10/13/86)

Just drop the *non*. Among the proposed components of this "non-nuclear defense" are: an X-ray laser which focuses radiation from a nuclear explosion into a beam of directed energy; a space-based gun used to shoot down enemy missiles with nuclear cartridges; and a space-based nuclear reactor used to power space-based SDI equipment. In addition, the Department of Energy's nuclear weapons program has received about $1 billion over the past four years for SDI research on nuclear-powered components.

66 *There was a line attributed to Nikolai Lenin, 'The road to America leads through Mexico.'* 99 (5/3/87)

At a press briefing, Gennady Gerasimov, spokesman for the Soviet Foreign Ministry, pointed to Lenin's collected works stacked on a nearby table and promised to eat his hat if anyone could find the "road to America" reference therein.

FALSE ALARM

Q: *"Mr. President, are Republican candidates going to be helped by how you did in Iceland?"*

A: *"I don't know of any hostages that are being held in Iceland."*

Q: *"No, Republican candidates—are Republican candidates going to be helped by how you did in Iceland?"*

A: *"Oh, I thought you said 'held.' I don't know. I'm going to find out between now and November 4th."* (10/15/86)

◄ UNFAMILIAR QUOTATION

Reagan on Reagan

"**W**here's the rest of me?" Ronald Reagan asked in *King's Row,* his most famous pre–January 20, 1981, acting job. Good question. If asked about makeup during his days in Hollywood, he'll deny ever using the stuff (that's not what his 1965 autobiography says). If asked about his role as Screen Actors Guild president, he'll tell any number of stories about standing up to the Hollywood commies in public (while conveniently editing out his role as FBI informant T-10, according to released FBI files). If asked about his military service, he'll hint at combat (airbrushing the fact that he merely provided voice-overs for training films). Indeed, the more one examines Reagan examining Reagan, the more one appreciates another line from *King's Row,* a line describing Reagan's character in the original novel: "That overhandsome face of Drake's was not a thinking face."

66 *By the time I got out of the Army Air Corps, all I wanted to do . . . was rest up a while, make love to my wife, and come up refreshed to a better job in an ideal world. (As it came out, I was disappointed in these postwar ambitions.)* 99 (*Where's the Rest of Me?* his 1965 autobiography)

The future commander-in-chief spent the war years commuting from his home to his Army Air Corps base, sleeping in his own bed next to his own wife every night.

66 *I know all the bad things that happened in that war. I was in uniform four years myself.* 99 (Interview with foreign journalists, 4/29/85)

"In costume" is more like it. Reagan spent World War II making Army training films at the Hal Roach Studios in Hollywood.

“In California, some time ago, a man beat a woman so savagely that her unborn child was born dead with a fractured skull. And the California state legislature unanimously passed a law that was signed by the then-Democratic Governor, signed a law that said that any man who so abuses a pregnant woman that he causes the death of her unborn child shall be charged with murder.” (10/7/84)

The "Democratic Governor" was actually a Republican Governor named Ronald Reagan.

“So, all this talk about that we did this [cause the deficit]— and all those years back over the last half-century when I was making speeches about deficit spending and all—the truth of the matter is, deficit spending was a deliberate practice of the party in power.” (2/10/86)

Putting aside the question of what was "deliberate practice," the "last half-century" of public speaking about deficit spending would have begun sometime in 1936. At that time, Reagan was a liberal Roosevelt Democrat whose only major public speaking forum was as a sportscaster for radio station WHO in Des Moines, Iowa. Most biographers trace the beginnings of Reagan's conservative politics (such as a concern for deficit spending) to 1952–53, the time of his marriage to Nancy Davis and his first speeches on behalf of General Electric.

“As Governor of the State of California, I had firsthand experience with the line-item veto, and found it necessary to keep spending in check and used the line-item veto on over 900 occasions to remove unnecessary spending from the budget.” (7/18/85)

According to Norma Lee, government publications reference

NEWS ITEM

Attacking the theories of British economist John Maynard Keynes, Reagan said they were "a legacy from a period when I was back in college studying economics." But Keynes's classic text, *The General Theory of Employment, Interest and Money* was first published in 1936, and Eureka College's most famous graduate received his B.A. in Economics in 1932. (*Wall Street Journal*, 12/12/86)

In November 1983 Reagan told a delegation of Israelis that he understood and sympathized with their cause, having seen for himself the devastation of the Holocaust while filming the liberation of the concentration camps. According to then Israeli prime minister Yitzhak Shamir, who was at the meeting, Reagan told them he had kept that film unshown for many years until he felt the moment was right and "showed it to a group of people who couldn't believe their eyes. From then on," said Reagan, "I was concerned for the Jewish people." Nazi-hunter Simon Wiesenthal reported that Reagan told him the same story.

However real his concern, Reagan's tale can't be true —although he served with the First Motion Picture Unit of the Army Air Corps, he never left the US during World War II.

librarian at the California State Library, Winston Crouch's 1981 study *California Government and Politics* has found only 206 budget items and 72 special appropriations act items eliminated between 1967 and 1975 by Governor Reagan's use of the line-item veto.

A DEFICIT OF ECONOMICS

When it comes to the economy, the President cites batches of selective statistics. Some are actually true: unemployment is below 7%, inflation is modest, corporate profits are recently on the rise. But in economics the Great Communicator is hardly the Great Calculator. Favorable numbers are "calculate[d] in his head," while he dismisses less favorable numbers produced by such dubious sources as the Departments of Treasury and Labor, and the Office of Management and Budget. To hear Reagan tell it, our raging deficits have been bridled, tax increases are something only Democrats do, and there really are homeless folks out there who enjoy sleeping on grates. The logic is clear: every economic tornado has a silver lining.

❝We look at the unemployed, and we incline to believe that this is the same group of people that have been sitting there helpless and hopeless throughout the entire recession. Seventy percent of the unemployed today have been unemployed seven weeks or less. **❞** (7/21/83)

DIPSY DOODLE

According to Labor Department figures, 41.1% of the nation's jobless in June had been unemployed for 15 weeks or longer, and only 26.1% of the unemployed had been jobless for five to 14 weeks. Accepting the Labor Department figures, the White House later explained that the President had been "calculating in his head" during the news conference.

❝I believe a lot of our ills are due to the minimum wage. I think we have priced a number of people and jobs out of existence by making the price for them too high. And if you go back, figures will bear out that every time the minimum wage increases, there is an increase, particularly in young people who have no job skill to bring to the market. **❞** (12/14/83)

A LESSON FROM HISTORY

Dr. Reagan should have asked for a second opinion. Data from the Bureau of Labor Statistics shows that there is no

"At one point, Representative Robert H. Michel, the House Republican leader, urged the President to indicate his support of a Federal insurance plan to cover catastrophic illnesses. Mr. Reagan responded by talking about a New York City welfare family living in a plush hotel at extravagant cost. Other leaders explained that catastrophic health insurance was not a welfare program, but Mr. Reagan reiterated his story about the welfare family."
(*New York Times*, 1/14/87)

A LESSON FROM HISTORY ▶

connection between minimum wage levels and youth unemployment figures. During Reagan's first two years in office this was quite apparent: the minimum wage in 1981 was $3.35/hr., up 25¢ from the previous year, and youth unemployment indeed went up from 17.8% to 19.6%, an increase of 10.1%. In 1982, however, the minimum wage did *not* change, yet youth unemployment still rose 23.2%. An extreme example of the disparity between fluctuations of minimum wage and youth unemployment occurred in 1950. The minimum wage jumped 87%, from 40¢/hr. to 75¢/hr., yet youth unemployment *dropped*, from 13.4% to 12.2%.

❝*Our budget cuts have been reductions in the increase planned in spending. We haven't come to some place where we're spending less than had been spent.* ❞ (3/13/84)

Many of Reagan's budget cuts have been reductions, period. Since January 1981, allocations for domestic programs such as school lunches, sewer construction and community block grants, and urban mass transit subsidies have shrunk in constant dollars, according to the Office of Management and Budget. In fact, some domestic programs—Aid to Families with Dependent Children, food stamps, job training, and park land acquisition, to name a few—received less funding in Fiscal Year 1984 than in Fiscal Year 1981 even without adjustments for inflation.

❝*It was more or less a standard acceptance in economics that the business cycle, so called, and the lean periods previous to that—what we now call recessions and depressions—when they did occur, that usually it was when government had gone beyond a certain point in the percentage of gross national product that it was taking.* ❞ (3/13/84)

This quaint pre-Keynesian theory is completely contradicted by the economic history of the United States during the last half-century. If Reagan's statement were true, the worst year of the Great Depression would have been 1944, when public sector expenditures accounted for 45.2% of the GNP, nearly twice the level in the recession year of 1982.

66 The truth is, if they wanted to even go back farther, back in the '60s, the early '60s, we had fewer people living below the poverty line than we had in the later '60s after the great War on Poverty got underway. 99 (3/21/84)

Truth is, of course, the first casualty of any war. According to the Census Bureau, there were 39.9 million Americans living below the poverty line in 1960, comprising 22.2% of the population. By 1965, the number of people living below the poverty line had *declined* to 33.2 million (17.3% of the population), and by the end of the decade, only 24.1 million Americans (12.1% of the population) were living in poverty.

66 And, granted, that blacks in this country had a higher rate of unemployment than whites at the time of the recession; their rate of recovery is faster than the rate of recovery for whites. 99 (6/14/84)

Actually, it's the other way around. Department of Labor statistics show that from 1982 to 1984, the unemployment rate for blacks decreased 16% (from 18.9% to 15.9%), while the unemployment rate for whites fell 24.4% (from 8.6% to 6.5%).

66 And so far, we have found repeatedly, and are still finding, that we have overestimated the deficits. . . . 99 (7/24/84)

Try underestimated. In three of Reagan's first four budgets,

HUH???

66[The poverty rate] has begun to decline, but it is still going up. 99 (10/7/84)

◄ WISHFUL THINKING DEPT.

deficit forecasts fell far short of the actual total. In Fiscal Year 1982, the estimate was $45 billion; the actual deficit was $110 billion. In Fiscal Year 1983, the estimate was $91.5 billion; the actual deficit was $195 billion. In Fiscal Year 1985, the estimate was $180 billion; the actual deficit was $202 billion.

A LESSON FROM HISTORY ➤

66 *We've had any number of tax increases over the last 50 years and we have had, regularly, deficits for 50 years, every year since World War II.* 99 (9/5/84)

The truth is, we've had eight budget surpluses since World War II, the last one in 1969.

FALSE ALARM

In late January 1987, House Speaker Jim Wright met with President Reagan to discuss the Clean Water Act, which Congress had just passed despite the President's objection to its expense. According to Wright, Reagan looked through his three-by-five cards and told the Speaker that "the bill was a pork-laden budget-buster that would cost $18 billion a year." "No, Mr. President," Wright replied, "it's $18 billion over nine years; that's a very long time."
(*Wash. Post*, 2/1/87)

66 *Take a look at the budgets I've submitted and look at the cuts that I've asked for and was not given.* 99 (9/11/84)

Those three budgets that Reagan had already submitted entailed expenditures slightly above $2.34 trillion. During the same fiscal years, Congress approved spending $2.37 trillion, about one percent more than what Reagan requested. Out of the $480 billion in red ink that those three budgets brought about, the portion wholly attributable to the cuts that Reagan asked for and was not given—$26 billion—comprised a mere 5.4% of the total deficit.

66 *Last year 600,000 new businesses were incorporated, and that was a record.* 99 (9/12/84)

Actually, the Index of Net Business Formation, which measures the ratio of new incorporations against failures (an index of 100 would indicate no net change), shows that the record has fallen from the high 130s in the late 1970s to a level of 121 in 1984–85.

"We have seen a $21 billion reduction in the deficit from last year, based mainly on the increased revenues the government is getting without raising taxes." (10/7/84)

But the government *did* raise taxes during Reagan's first term. Four times in fact. The biggest tax increase of the four, the Tax Equity and Fiscal Responsibility Act, which was passed over Reagan's live body in 1982, raised about $40 billion each year, principally by closing loopholes in personal and corporate income taxes.

"Well, we decontrolled oil prices. It was one of the first things we did." (10/16/84)

WISHFUL THINKING DEPT.

Reagan was merely the last of several presidents who worked to eliminate price controls on oil. Responding to Gerald Ford's call for total decontrol, in 1975 Congress established a seven-year schedule for the automatic phasing-out of controls. By the end of the Carter administration, phased decontrol was about 75% complete. Upon taking office, Reagan ordered the immediate lifting of all remaining price controls, which would otherwise have expired September 1981. In essence, Reagan administered the *coup de grace* to a program that had only six more months to live.

"This budget shows, moreover, that eliminating the deficit is possible . . . without *cutting into legitimate programs for the poor and the elderly."* (2/5/86)

On the contrary, Reagan's 1987 budget request showed that eliminating legitimate programs for the poor and the elderly is possible without making a big dent in the deficit. Not only did the administration propose in this budget to cut every low-income entitlement program, it proposed terminating, among others, the Legal Services Corporation, the Work

"What we have found in this country, and maybe we're more aware of it now, is one problem that we've had, even in the best of times, and that is the people who are sleeping on the grates, the homeless who are homeless, you might say, by choice."
(1/31/84)

WISHFUL THINKING DEPT. ➤

Incentive Program, housing assistance for the elderly and handicapped, and the emergency food and shelter program —fourteen low-income programs in all. And the budget still forecast a deficit of $144 billion.

"The truth of the matter is this: in need of immediate help are . . . 4% at best of all the farmers in the United States; 96% do not have any liquidity problems." (3/6/85)

The truth of the matter is more than triple Reagan's figure. Yes, 4.4.% of all family-sized commercial farms were "technically insolvent" in 1984, but by 1985 that figure had risen to 6.3%. And, according to the Agriculture Department's January 1985 report, another 7.4% of these farms were in "extreme financial difficulty" and their short-term prospects were likely to worsen because "land prices will decline further in 1985." So a total of 13.7% of family-sized farms had liquidity problems, not 4%.

"[The Job Corps] is a vital program . . . in keeping with the American spirit of helping others to reach their full potential, the spirit that has sustained our nation from its very founding. . . . Nancy and I send everyone present our best wishes for future success." (Washington Post, 4/22/85)

Nancy's best wishes notwithstanding, Reagan's 1986 budget proposed that the Job Corps be abolished.

"You can't show me a time in history when a major tax cut did not result in greater revenue." (New York Times, 7/11/85)

How about the time after the Reagan tax cuts became law? Measured in constant 1982 dollars, revenues fell substantially in Fiscal Years 1982 and 1983, from $642 billion in Fiscal

Year 1981 (Carter's last budget) to a low of $576 billion in Fiscal Year 1983, a 10% drop. Revenues did rebound modestly the following year, equalling the Fiscal Year 1982 level of $618 billion, according to the Office of Management and Budget.

❝ *The current system rewards rich tax states with big budgets and high taxes. You people who've been responsible and kept your budgets low don't receive an equal benefit. That's no way to run a federal tax system.* **❞** (9/18/85)

While individuals may pay higher taxes because they're wealthy, that doesn't mean high-tax states themselves are rich. Quite the contrary, high-tax states like Massachusetts, New York, and Pennsylvania have high tax rates because they have a disproportionate number of the nation's poor and disadvantaged.

❝ *When Eisenhower left office, his budget was smaller than when he started. The spending line was actually lower.* **❞** (Quoted in *The Triumph of Politics* by David Stockman)

No, under Eisenhower the spending line actually went up. According to the Office of Management and Budget, Eisenhower's 1961 budget was $355 billion (measured in 1982 constant dollars), $24 billion higher than his 1954 budget of $330.9 billion.

❝ *. . . the best economic expansion this country's seen in a quarter of a century.* **❞** (4/9/86)

According to Commerce Department figures, it's been the most anemic recovery since 1960. In the four key categories that gauge overall economic performance—real GNP, productivity, real after-tax income, and industrial production—

the present recovery, which began at the end of 1982, ranks dead last in comparison with the other four recoveries of this quarter century.

FALSE ALARM ➡

❝*Now, if you took all the books of regulations and rules in the Tax Code, the Income Tax Code, and put them all on a shelf, the shelf would be 57 feet long to hold all of them.*❞ (7/23/86)

Reagan is stretching the truth here—by about 56½ feet. The 1982 Internal Revenue section of the United States Code, combined with all of the additions and revisions enacted through December 1985, spans six inches from beginning to end.

❝*I just read this morning in the paper about a needy family in New York that is being put up in a hotel and the cost to welfare, just for the rent of the hotel, runs $37,000 a year. And I wonder why somebody doesn't build them a house for $37,000.*❞ (11/19/86)

To begin with, the $37,000 "rent" payment included a food allowance administered by the hotel operator. But the Emergency Assistance program was designed to provide only short-term relief—food and temporary shelter—for destitute families. This program contains no provision for the construction of permanent housing for the poor. (On June 15, 1987, the Reagan administration informed Congress that it *opposed* a bill to allow for such construction because it would put the Department of Health and Human Services "into the housing construction and acquisition business [which is] clearly inappropriate for the department.") As to why low-income housing is in such scarce supply, Reagan need not look beyond his own budgets. Funding for low-income public housing has been cut by over 70% since 1980, and his 1987 budget contained no money for new public housing.

"There will be no tax increase in the 100th Congress."
(3/24/87)

But according to Treasury Secretary James A. Baker III, the Reagan administration's 1988 budget contains "about $6.1 billion in revenues that I think it's fair to say probably represents [increased] taxes."

"The increase in inflation has been in sort of fringe items like toothpaste and Kleenex and things of that kind. . . . [Higher oil prices have] been relatively stable. That's not a contributing factor at this time." (4/24/87)

Secretary Baker, who sat silently by as the President made his remarks, had earlier that day released Consumer Price Index figures which, he said, "reflect[ed] primarily something that we have been saying to be the case for quite some time, and that is an increase in oil prices."

"Most of us believe that the dollar should remain stable. It could be within reason that there could still be some lowering of the value in relation to other currencies." (6/11/87)

Those who believed the dollar should remain stable and not be used as a weapon against other nations' economies included the heads of the seven nations present at the 1987 economic summit in Venice. Reagan's statement came during a press conference twenty-four hours after the summit's end and sent the dollar sliding downward on foreign exchange markets within minutes. Embarrassed White House aides corrected the President within fifteen minutes: "He's referring to other forces [that affect the dollar], but he wants stability," said White House spokesman Marlin Fitzwater.

The Name Game

WHAT HE SAID	WHAT HE MEANT
Andrea	CBS reporter Lesley Stahl
Sugar Ray and Mrs. Ray	Sugar Ray Leonard and Mrs. Leonard
" . . . great pleasure to welcome Prime Minister Lee Kuan Yew and Mrs. Yew to Singapore"	" . . . great pleasure to welcome Prime Minister Lee Kuan Yew and Mrs. Lee to Washington"
the people of Bolivia	the people of Brazil
Chairman Moe	Chairman Doe of Liberia
Princess David	Princess Diana
Emmett Lazarus	poet Emma Lazarus
John Philpot Curran	Irish orator James Philpot Curran
Don Rickles	Oklahama Senator Don Nickles
"Don"	William Ruckelshaus
Ed Nitze	his arms control negotiator Paul H. Nitze
Mr. Mayor	HUD Secretary Samuel Pierce

ALL IN THE FAMILY

Question: What's worse than a president who habitually gets into trouble with embarrassing off-the-cuff remarks? Answer: An entire administration with the same problem. Reagan has surrounded himself with some of the most audacious foot-in-mouth artists ever to have stumbled into Washington, a group apparently eager to show the boss that "imitation is the sincerest form of flattery." Where else but in the Reagan administration would a cabinet officer boast that his advisory commission was made up of "a black, a woman, two Jews, and a cripple"? Only in the Reagan administration would a senior White House adviser state for the record that "people go to soup kitchens because the food is free and . . . that's easier than paying for it." Such Archie Bunkeresque wit and wisdom dissolved into less humorous versions when it came to Irangate, which opened up whole new frontiers in imitative imprecision.

J. Peter Grace, head of President Reagan's Private Sector Survey on Cost Control in the Federal Government, told the American Feed Manufacturers Association's 1982 meeting in Dallas that the federal food stamp program is "basically a Puerto Rican program." *UPI* reported that Mr. Grace also said that all the Puerto Ricans in New York City are on food stamps. Mr. Grace said he believed he said "almost all" Puerto Ricans. (*Wall Street Journal*, 6/1/82)

"I don't know of any authoritative figures that there are hungry children. I've heard a lot of anecdotal stuff, but I haven't heard any authoritative figures. . . .**"** Presidential adviser Edwin Meese III (12/8/83)

The General Accounting Office (GAO) and the US Department of Agriculture (USDA) had issued reports in May and June 1983, respectively, documenting significant increases in the numbers of individuals needing food and nutritional assistance. The GAO went to 28 emergency food centers and

HUH???

"We have permitted our naval capability to deteriorate. At the same time we are better than we were a few years ago." Secretary of Defense Caspar Weinberger (3/4/82)

PROBLEM SOLVING

"If you want to know how to pray for the President, pray that anyone directly around him gets saved or gets out." White House liaison for religious affairs Carolyn Sundseth (1/31/84)

NEWS ITEM

R. Leonard Vance, director of health standards at OSHA, told a House subcommittee in late March 1984 that the documents it sought in an investigation of possible misconduct had been destroyed when his dogs threw up on them.
(*Common Cause* magazine, July/Aug. 1984)

❝As we look at the problems of our blacks, all we have to do is look at our sports page to see who are the best nourished in the country.**❞** Dr. George Graham, one of the 13 members of Reagan's commission on hunger, in 1982. (*The Economist,* 1/14/84)

discovered that "in almost all cases, the emergency food centers were serving more than in the past," and that "an unmet need remains." After examining 9 emergency food centers around the country, Social and Scientific Systems, Inc., reported to the USDA that "increases in the number of food boxes distributed ranged from 15[%] to more than several hundred [percent], with the norm being in the range of 60 to 75%."

❝The United States is not mining the harbors of Nicaragua.**❞** Secretary of Defense Caspar Weinberger (4/8/84)

According to an article published in *Time* magazine two weeks later, ". . . an inter-agency committee representing State, Defense, and the CIA by the end of 1983 agreed on a package of measures, including mining. The President approved the package. . . ."

❝Spending for food stamps is way, way up under the Reagan administration. AFDC is up under the Reagan administration and I am not going to be found wrong on that. I am sure of my facts . . .**❞** George Bush (10/11/84)

Sure enough, his facts are wrong. Figures from the Office of Management and Budget indicate that food stamp spending *dropped* from $12.485 billion in Fiscal Year 1981 to $10.764 billion in Fiscal Year 1984. During that same period, welfare spending fell from $9.434 billion to $7.201 billion (all figures adjusted to constant 1983 dollars).

❝The President is the one who saved the Social Security system. We came in and found it was bankrupt. The thing you're talking about was imposed by Congress and has been corrected by this administration.**❞** George Bush (10/11/84)

The "thing you're talking about" was an assertion by an elderly man that 500,000 people had lost their disability pensions under the current administration. In fact, Congress had nothing to do with the Reagan administration's removal of 200,000 people from the rolls of disability insurance, and the federal courts ordered that these benefits be restored.

"Seven new Trident submarines have been built since we

NEWS ITEM

Marianne Mele Hall, confirmed in mid-1985 as chairman of the Copyright Royalty Tribunal, listed herself on a Senate questionnaire as "co-author" of a book called *Foundations of Sand.* The book asserts that American blacks "insist on preserving their jungle freedoms," argues in favor of segregated schools, and opposes welfare as "subsidized procreation." Following the revelations about *Foundations of Sand,* Hall demoted herself from "co-author" to "editor," explaining that as an editor, "you don't need to understand . . . what you are reading." (*The New Republic,* 5/27/85)

ABOUT FACE!

Secretary of the Navy John Lehman:
"There very definitely has been a shift in emphasis to make it clear that we will be providing supporting fire to the Lebanese armed forces. That is not linked to specific incoming fire against the marines at the airport." (2/14/84)

Pentagon chief spokesman Michael Burch:
"We're not providing fire in direct support of the Lebanese armed forces." (2/14/84)

LITTLE KNOWN FUN FACT ➤

came to Washington. 99 Secretary of Defense Caspar Weinberger (2/7/85)

Replace "built" with "completed" and Weinberger would have been correct. As it was, work on five of the seven Trident submarines had already begun before January 20, 1981, the day of Reagan's inauguration. According to the Navy, one was begun in 1976, two in 1977, one in 1979, and one a day before Reagan took office.

66 You don't have many suspects who are innocent of a crime. That's contradictory. If a person is innocent of a crime, then he is not a suspect. 99 Attorney General Edwin Meese III (*US News and World Report,* 10/14/85)

Under the American system of justice, a suspect is innocent until proven guilty. Would Attorney General Meese apply his revised standard to himself? For as of July 1987, he was a suspect in three different investigations: first, a special prosecutor was looking into conflict-of-interest charges arising out of Meese's actions during the Wedtech scandal; second, Meese's own Justice Department was inquiring into his delay of a probe into Southern Air Transport (a private airline involved in shipments of arms to the contras); and, third, yet another Justice Department inquiry was probing Meese's actions during his initial investigation of the Iran-Contra scandal.

66 [Women are] not . . . going to understand throw-weights or what is happening in Afghanistan or what is happening in human rights. . . . Some women will, but most women . . . would rather read the human interest stuff of what happened. . . . [Mrs. Reagan] doesn't get into throw-weights or war-heads or methods of transporting these warheads. 99 White House chief of staff Donald Regan (11/18/85)

❝*There is no single leader that has more credibility than Arturo Cruz, certainly in this country, and, I would say, in Nicaragua. Nobody's irreplaceable, but he comes as close as you can get.***❞** Assistant Secretary of State Elliott Abrams (*Washington Post,* 2/19/87)

Less than one month later, on March 9, 1987, Cruz resigned, whereupon Abrams changed his mind: "The resistance does not depend on any individual leader and in fact is now moving toward a larger and broad directorate."

❝ *. . . [I] still don't know anything about the mechanisms by which money was transferred from private groups that have been raising it, to the contras. . . . We don't engage—I mean the State Department's function in this has not been to raise money, other than to try to raise it from Congress.***❞** Assistant Secretary of State Elliott Abrams (11/25/86)

Abrams had previously, in fact, personally solicited representatives of the Sultan of Brunei (an oil-producing nation located in the South China Sea) for a $10 million contribution for the contras. Abrams later told the Iran-Contra hearings that his November statement was "perhaps misleading."

❝*We do not engage in, nor did we really know anything about this private network.***❞** Assistant Secretary of State Elliott Abrams to the Tower Commission (12/19/86)

In testimony before the House and Senate Iran-Contra committees, retired Army General John Singlaub described Abrams as "the principal contact for activities in Central America." Former U.S. ambassador to Costa Rica Lewis Tambs, in testimony before the same committees, said that Abrams had chaired a committee that directed him to help the contras open a "southern front" in Nicaragua.

NEWS ITEM

In August 1986, *Washington Post* reporter Bob Woodward broke a story describing an elaborate administration campaign of deception designed to demoralize Libyan leader Muammar Qaddafi. Woodward quoted from a memorandum by then–National Security Adviser John Poindexter outlining a scheme that "combines real and illusionary events—through a disinformation program—with the basic goal of making Qaddafi think there is a high degree of internal opposition to him within Libya, that his key trusted aides were disloyal, that the United States is about to move against him militarily."

NEWS ITEM

Former Secretary of the Interior James Watt said that he had never heard of the Holocaust until he became Secretary of the Interior. (*The New Republic,* 2/25/85)

NEWS ITEM

After being heckled at the third International AIDS Conference in Washington for calling for mandatory testing for the disease, Vice-President George Bush, unaware that the microphone was still on, said to a colleague, "Who was that? Some gay group?" (6/1/87)

NEWS ITEM

The director of the US Information Agency, Charles Z. Wick, told columnist William Safire and *New York Times* reporter Jane Perlez in December 1983 that he had never secretly tape-recorded his office telephone conversations. A few days later, it was revealed that Wick had, in fact, lied to Safire and Perlez. Wick admitted recording what he called "a small percentage" of such calls without informing the other party. (*New York Times,* 12/28/83)

66 . . . *What you've got to understand is we were barred from being involved with the contras and we kept away from that.* 99 CIA director William J. Casey (12/19/86)

Apparently Casey kept away from the ban, rather than the banned. In his testimony before congressional committees investigating the Iran-Contra scandal (5/7/87), retired general Richard V. Secord, a major operative in the network supplying private aid to the contras, said, "I believe I was receiving support from the director of central intelligence. . . . We received some support from a senior CIA officer in Honduras." Two weeks later (5/20/87), contra leader Adolfo Calero, testifying before the same committees, confirmed that Casey knew of assistance provided by Secord and N.S.C. aide Lieutenant Colonel Oliver North: "Yes . . . [I told Casey] how we were acquiring more weapons, and . . . he was hoping that this support would be forthcoming."

66 *People who don't stand out in the sun—it doesn't affect them.* 99 Secretary of the Interior Donald Hodel (*Wall Street Journal,* 5/29/87)

Secretary Hodel was arguing that the increased risk of cancer from growing ultraviolet radiation (due to a depleted ozone layer) was not a serious threat and could be offset by the use of sunglasses, hats, and sunscreen. David Doniger, a lawyer for the Natural Resources Defense Council, calculated that the cost of implementing Hodel's proposed solution for every American would be $10 billion a year (or ten times what industry predicts a freeze on ozone-depleting chemicals would cost over a decade). And what of damage to crops, livestock, and marine life? "It is very hard," Doniger told the *Wall Street Journal,* "to get animals to wear hats and sunglasses."

Office of Management and Budget Director David Stockman told a Canadian official that a national emissions-control program would cost American tax-payers "$6,000 per pound of fish" (*Wash. Post,* 10/17/83). Scoffed a Library of Congress spokesman, "We have a hard enough time taking a census of people; we haven't tried to take one of fish." Beyond that, Stockman's cost-benefit analysis also errs by assuming that only New England fish would benefit materially from acid rain controls. According to the Izaak Walton League, there is irrefutable evidence of acid rain damage to other wildlife, forests, farmlands, and buildings in various locations around the country, such as southern Appalachia, the upper Midwest, and parts of California.

ADD YOUR OWN

" _____
_____
_____
_____
_____
_____
_____ "

" _____
_____
_____
_____
_____
_____ " (   )

" _____
_____
_____ " (   )

" _____
_____
_____
_____
_____ " (   )

" _____
_____
_____
_____
_____
_____
_____ " (   )

" _____
_____
_____ " (   )

"_____
_____
_____
_____" (   )

"_____
_____" (   )

"_____
_____
_____
_____" (   )

"_____
_____
_____
_____" (   )

"_____
_____
_____" (   )

"_____
_____
_____
_____
_____" (   )

"_____
_____" (   )

"_____
_____
_____
_____
_____
_____
_____
_____"

MARK GREEN, president of the Democracy Project, is the author or editor of twelve books, including *Who Runs Congress?* and is a frequent commentator on television and radio. He was the Democratic nominee for the United States Senate from New York in 1986.

GAIL MACCOLL is a freelance writer and editor whose credits include *The Official Preppy Handbook* and *Items from Our Catalog.*